Globalization Issues and Challenges (An Overview)

By

Shabeer Ahmad Bhat

CREATESPACE
INDEPENDENT PUBLISHING
PLATFORM

No human work is perfect and free from flaws. Therefore, if the readers point out any omissions or mistakes, we shall be pleased and thankful to them and see that the corrections are made in the next edition as appropriate

ISBN-13: 978-1499643695
ISBN-10: 1499643691

Globalization Issues and Challenges: An Overview

Published by:
CREATESPACE
INDEPENDENT PUBLISHING
PLATFORM

Publishing Country:
India

Publishing Date
22 May 2014
Designed By:
Aijaz Ahmad Bhat
Library Assistant
GMC, Srinagar
Contact: salfiaijazmlis@gmail.com

Globalization Issues and Challenges
(An Overview)

SHABEER AHMAD BHAT

PUBLISHED BY

CREATESPACE
INDEPENDENT PUBLISHING
PLATFORM

Acknowledgement

My sincere gratitude to the following people without whom this would not have been possible:

Javeed Ahmad (Sociologist SKIMS), Primary Advisor for going through multiple drafts of my work in excruciating detail. For being incredibly accessible both in-person and via email and responding to 'crisis' emails at odd hours telling me I had nothing to worry about. For answering all my questions, however minuscule and ridiculous they may have been.

Bilal Ahmad Bhat, for offering insightful comments and relevant feedback and for the encouragement to get through this. Kulsum Raja Nayak, for his painstaking effort and dedication toward ensuring that this final product was of top quality. For being the most motivational person I know. For the support at all times and being the recipient of those occasional 'crisis' emails as well. For the constructive feedback that was extremely helpful in the writing process. For the wealth of knowledge that I had the privilege of accessing and someone I would like to emulate one day. For being a role model.

And of course, my family Members like my brother Muzamil Shaheen Bhat, My sisters Andli and Tanveera Lalie and my father and mother Ab Razak Bhat and Muneera Akhter without whom I would not be here in the university of Kashmir, and last, but certainly not least, my friends (particularly Dr. Mudasir Ahmad Lone for taking time out to edit and read through my work in so much detail and for his insightful feedback) and suitemates for getting me through the worst of it. I am humbled by you all.

SHABEER AHMAD BHAT

Table of Contents

Preface

This book is an outcome of four years hardworking efforts taking by the respective author. All the period which I spend in the University of Kashmir for educational purposes the process of globalization was becoming my area of interest slowly which compels me to read and write something intensively about this particular topic. Keeping in view the dynamic and significant nature of globalization this book was written in this book various issues and challenges which are confronting modern societies were highlighted at both macro and micro levels.

In the first chapter of the book initiatives have been taken to analyze and interpret the experiences of the world with the process of globalization. However theoretical frameworks have been taken from different pioneering works like the works of Anthony Giddens and Immunal Walleristein to make ideas theoretical sound and practically relevant.

The second chapter of the book is an effort to show how the process is confronting the democratic and trade policies of all the countries of the world In this chapter theoretical knowledge with live evidences have been combined in a coherent manner so that things can become easy to communicate and understand for all eager readers and writers.

Chapter 3rd is mainly concerned with conflict and experiences of localities in post modern industrialized and capitalist societies. Besides this globalization in general has been defined in light of various social thinkers along with this explanation various sub themes have been touched and interpreted sociologically, which may include Religion, Economics and financial globalization and globalization from religious point of view.

Chapter fourth is mainly concerned with the emerging issues related with children, in this chapter efforts were initiated to look into the causes and consequences of child labor in the global village, attempts were also undertaken to highlight the various safeguards for the protection of children rights in the process of globalization and recommendations were given to solve the child associated problems Sociologically and scientifically at macro level.

Chapter fifth is focused to the gender related problems in the global context, in this chapter various challenges were highlighted associated with women folk which may include status of women in work places, in family, and in other primary and secondary social institutions of modern societies. Ultimately the main focus of this chapter is to show how the process of globalization is responsible for deteriorating the status of women in rural societies in the world.

Chapter sixth is an attempt to show the emergence of conflict between great civilizations of the world in this chapter analysis of ideological conflicts and differences between haves and have not have been studied. The focus of this chapter is to resolve conflict between nations which are existing un the world especially 1989 onwards live examples and evidences were studied and interpreted scientifically and Sociologically to make this work an objective and valuable one.

Chapter seven is concerned with tourism in general in the age of globalization and tourism in particular in the Arab world in relation with globalization. In this chapter content analysis as the source of data collection was employed to get the exact tourist flow from other parts of the world to the Arab world and it was founded that pilgrimage tourism is emerging as a source of income for the Arab countries at macro level. However it was found that this process of pilgrimage tourism along with general tourism can flow day by day but it is hindrances by terrorism which is spreading in this part of the world like anything.

Chapter eighth is a focused chapter on the environment and globalization relationship. In this chapter problems which are associated with environmental degradation were highlighted However attention was also given to this fact that environment and ecological imbalance is mainly caused by the more developed nations of the world because they are the producers of poison gases like O2 Methane and smog in a huge quantity. In this chapter various protocols and treaties which are signed in and among the nations for environmental protection were also interpreted and their role and implication were also studied.

Chapter 1
Globalization a Comparative analyses in the World

Introduction

Over the last three decades, social scientists have taken the fact of globalization – the increasing interconnectedness of the world as a complex system – for granted. The processes of globalization, including its often negative consequences, have appeared to be inevitable and all embracing. No society, however small and remote, could escape entanglement with such global cultural, political and economic processes. Any sociological analysis of a single society, region, city or village that did not take into account the global context was seen to be inadequate. Yet suddenly from September 2008 the unfolding of a global economic crisis that appeared to fan outwards from the problems in the American housing market to undermine the financial stability of whole societies such as Iceland brought into question many of our comfortable assumptions about the world and its economic foundations. There were rumors in the corridors of university social science faculties that the facts of globalization were perhaps not as secure as we had been led to believe. Why had economists in general failed to understand the fragility of the global financial system? Do we need as a result new perspectives on globalization? Will globalization as we know it come to an end? However, by the middle of 2009 the financial world appeared to have achieved some equilibrium and by September 2009 there were signs of a recovery in Europe and the United States which followed the recovery in Asia on the heels. A study commissioned by the

United Nations (2009) revealed that there are deep and systemic problems with the global economy, the most important of which was social inequality. The Report recommended long-term solutions in addition to short-term stabilization measures. These questions about the economic character of globalization represent simply one.

PROSPECTS FOR A NEW SOCIOLOGY OF GLOBALIZATION

Globalization East and West dimension of our approach to globalization which we consider from the perspective of the East and from the West. Although the financial crisis has already brought misery to many thousands of families in the developing world, we see new democratic opportunities within this crisis, but we also detect the need for some major rethinking of the actual nature of globalization. In the wake of the global financial crisis of 2008 which developed into a global economic crisis in 2009 with a bleak prognosis for the future (World Bank, 2009; United Nations, 2009), many writers are understandably blaming globalization for our economic difficulties. The extreme turbulence in the global economy and the snowballing of the crisis from one country to another have indeed raised questions about the sustainability of the world economic architecture. Is globalization – viewed as the unbridled free market at play – to be replaced by a return to managed or state-centered economic systems? While some commentators recommend protectionism as the most appropriate strategy to stabilize the global economy, other economists suggest a comprehensive rearrangement of the global economic system as the only long-term solution. A leading economist, Jagdish Baghwati (2007), was confident that further economic globalization will in fact be the cure, but the challenges that the world faces are largely rooted in the gap between economic and political institutions. While the world has in economic terms become sufficiently global to emerge as a loosely integrated global economic system, the global economy is not matched by the institutional development of a global polity. Inadequate and ineffective coordination between the global economy and regulatory institutions has given rise to the possibility of a deep and prolonged economic crisis extending into the future, despite President Obama's huge injection of funding into the American economy as a recovery strategy. Yet in both the diagnosis and the cure of the crisis, policy-makers, as well as large sections of the public, continue to equate globalization only with economic globalization. It is imperative that we broaden our perspective on globalization as a multidimensional process in which economic globalization is only one of the important factors. Globalization, viewed as a macro-social process, inevitably gives rise to questions about its future. Do social processes come to an end, or do they change course according to newly emerging social and economic conditions?

If we highlight the structural or systemic features of globalization alone, then the conclusion becomes inescapable. All systems - ecological and economic - are in a constant process of transformation and change. However, if globalization is seen as an all-encompassing social condition, the processes of globalization will continue to shape the lives of people in the foreseeable future both at the level of everyday reality and at the level of social systems. The globalization process must change and adapt to newly emerging conditions if we are to plan more effectively for global pandemics, financial crises, economic inequality and imbalances in population movements through migration. As various writers in the last decade of the twentieth century celebrated the coming of the age of globalization, they also stressed the plurality of the processes of globalization, and hence it was important to speak in the plural of "globalizations". In the first decade of the twenty-first century, other critics have started to talk about the possibility of some disengagement from globalization, referring to new concepts such as "assemblage" and "re-assemblage" to describe the possibilities of disconnecting and disaggregating the components of global systems. In addition, it is well known that the processes of globalization do not preclude certain parallel processes such as regionalization and that in fact the two are interrelated (Therborn and Khondker, 2006). Disengagement from globalization, entailing the temporary repositioning and redirecting of trade flows, is often an aspect of the trading strategies of nations and regions, but these processes should not be seen as incompatible with globalization. Although globalization cannot be seen as an example of Max Weber's irreversible "iron cage", it is perhaps better described in the words of Ernest Gellner as a "rubber cage". While nation-states have some degree of flexibility in relation to globalization, they cannot enjoy complete independence from global constraints. Will a new global catastrophe make people want to return to the secure boundaries of the nation-state? We are skeptical about the openness of social systems – at least in the medium term. While the idea of a "borderless world" has become somewhat tired as a result of excessive overuse, we see the erection of walls and fences separating borders between nations as evidence that the porosity of state boundaries should not be exaggerated. The world is only borderless for the privileged few, but for the great majority of humanity it is a tightly bordered and highly regulated world. We see as a consequence of such "gated communities", "gated" or "walled" countries, the emergence of what Bryan Turner (2007) calls the "enclave society", characterizing modernity in terms of immobility in opposition to the claims supporting ideas about global mobility and "flexible citizenship" (Ong, 1999). With the growth of widespread urban terrorism from New York to Mumbai, we believe that the need for securitization by modern states will limit the possibilities for human mobility and porous state borders. We follow Roland Robertson (2007) in believing that transparency and surveillance are simply the opposite sides of the same coin of this global condition. Given these assumptions about the emphasis on security as a priority concern of the modern state, we need to ask whether – environmental, political, or biological attack on a state or states – will bring an end to globalization as we know it. Such a catastrophe would not be confined to the developed world. Based on recent trends, most of the future pandemics of global scope would originate from the developing world. The 9/11 attacks on New York and Washington and the fear of terrorism took a heavy toll on tourism and the travel industries but obviously did not halt global tourism. Soon after the attack, one commentator prematurely declared that globalization was over. Because of the physical impact on Wall Street in New York City, the financial market stalled temporarily but bounced back in full vigor in a matter of weeks. Yet 9/11 has become a template for understanding other acts of terrorism. The attacks in London in July 2005 were immediately labeled as the "7/7 terrorist attacks" and the Mumbai terrorist attacks on 26 November 2008 were equally quickly labeled as the "26/11" attack or "India's 9/11". The deeper processes of globalization did not rest for a moment as a result of such devastating attacks, despite the scale of the trauma, the collective sense of fear and the prospect of military conflict between India and Pakistan. The 9/11 attack itself could of course be seen as a global attack in its perceived causes, methods, and strategies as well as its consequences. Modern terrorism is a menace to the normal functioning of civil society, rather like "low intensity wars", pestilence and pandemics, but the consequence so far has not been to halt or even necessarily to transform globalization. These disturbances are indeed the unpleasant underbelly of globalization that is often masked by the alluring world of global consumerism, tourism, popular culture and sport. We are throughout this study struck by the deeply contradictory nature of globalization. In this discussion we argue that globalization points to the contradictory processes of wall removing and wall building. The modern world witnessed the dismantling of the Berlin Wall as part of the collapse of the Soviet system and at the same time there was the emergence a new ideological Berlin Wall – between the East and the West – as a negation of the historical transactions and exchanges between cultures and civilizations over the centuries. The international relations perspective of Samuel Huntington, who coined the phrase "the clash of civilizations" in which world-views, cultures and values remain incommensurable, has not been borne out either by recent history or by the opinion polls. A recent book based on Gallup surveys, where the authors analyzed 50,000 face-to-face interviews in 40 Muslim countries, found that only 7 per cent justified the 9/11 terrorist attacks in terms of political reasons. The study also found that what Muslims most admired about the West was its technological progress and its democratic politics. What both Muslims, and a large number of Americans, admired least about the West was its moral decay and the breakdown of traditional values (Esposito and Mogahed, 2008). Although in everyday usage and in political rhetoric, as well as in some popular social science discussions, phrases such as "East versus West" and "the Christian world versus the Islamic world" are freely used, we argue that such simple binaries fail to capture the actual complexities of the contemporary world. One of the deeper consequences of globalization is in fact the obliteration of such differences. Although our study is called *Globalization East and West*, our main aim is to question such traditional geographical divisions. Contrary to other popular views, the world has not become flat; far from it. Globalization has rendered the world more complex and hence more difficult to understand, and therefore we need to abandon simple slogans about globalization such as "the world is flat". In an interview on CNN's chat show *Global Public Square* hosted by Fareed Zakaria and aired on 28 September 2008, the Chinese Prime Minister Wen Jiabao, not only referred to Adam Smith's *The Causes of the Wealth of Nations* as a guide to economic development, but also alluded to the *Theory of Moral Sentiments* in order to buttress the importance of ethical considerations in a market-driven world. He stressed moral questions and raised issues relating to social equity and justice. Whether Marxist idealism can coexist with market-driven capitalism is an issue that only the future of China's development can settle. In fact one could see the spread and survival of the socialist ideas of Karl Marx and Friedrich Engels, and their continuing hold on the global, as a concrete historical example of globalization. However, Wen identified Marcus Aurelius's *Meditations* rather than Marx's *Capital* as the principal inspiration for his moral and ethical position. Surprisingly, he did not quote from either Confucius or Mencius. In fact the Chinese leadership is slowly abandoning references to Marxist-Leninism and favouring a restoration of neo-Confucianism as a state ideology with its powerful emphasis on respect for order and social peace. It is far from self-evident that globalization will bring about the hegemony of neo-liberal ideas as the necessary underpinning of a market economy. Another feature of globalization is that the leadership of global processes is constantly changing. Several writers have, for instance, commented on the shifting centers of global economic power. In the theories of Immanuel Wallerstein (1974), the core economies of the world system in the past were never permanent – their fates changed with historical circumstances. In the contemporary world, the economic powers of the twentieth century – North America, Europe and Japan as represented in the G7 and G8 (with Russia) – are increasingly being forced to take notice of the emerging BRIC countries (Brazil, Russia, India and China). The rise of these new centres of economic power is illustrated by the fact that, of the 500 firms listed by the business magazine *Fortune*, 62 are from the BRIC countries (*The Economist*, 20 September 2008, p. 3). Some of these firms, such as Lenovo of China and Tata of India, have also displayed remarkable creativity and innovative styles. Can sociology explain globalization? While books on globalization grow like conceptual mushrooms, the quality of theories of globalization is often poor, and research often scanty and inadequate. In fact, is there a distinctly *sociological* perspective on globalization? Our answer is affirmative. However, most sociological theory deals with micro–macro relations but typically within the nation-state, the region or the city. There seems to be some difficulty in thinking analytically about global processes, despite the encouragement and example of a minority of sociologists such as Roland Robertson. The main exceptions showing how we might develop genuinely sociological perspectives are probably George Ritzier on McDonaldization, Ulrich Beck on the risk society and cosmopolitanism, Anthony Giddens on distantiation theory, and Manuel Castells on the network society. From each of these sociological viewpoints, they make important contributions to our understanding of some selective aspects of globalization but do not provide a complete or comprehensive picture. Castells's work, however, makes significant strides in linking the role of communication in a networked society of capitalism and outlines several critical processes in which globalization can be challenged. Furthermore, he does not prematurely make a judgment about the outcome of globalization, because he sees the control and ownership of the global media as the outcome of endless struggles between various elites. There is nevertheless a lot of theoretical speculation but little genuine research. For example John Urry (2000) talked about "sociology beyond societies", but just how mobile are the majority of people? How many people globally at least make one international flight per year? How many have international holidays, own a holiday home, have a passport, migrate to secure a higher income, marry a foreign person, or send their children overseas for education? What little research we have suggests people have strong subjective ties to their local town, city or region and do not exhibit strong cosmopolitan values.

What are the implications of high mobility for elites? How does this impact on the concept of the self? Under what conditions could we anticipate the emergence of cosmopolitan identities? Do only cultural elites qualify for cosmopolitan status? What about the underclass of globe-trotting, undocumented, casual workers? Is there cosmopolitanism from below as well as from above? Against the processes of geographical mobility, the crisis of terrorism and the emergence of new wars – which are also genuine examples of globalization – have produced a new emphasis on security, surveillance and the sovereignty of the state. Unfortunately, the outbreak of a pandemic, which many public health officials believe is inevitable, would certainly place significant limits on human mobility. The swine flu pandemic of 2009 may be less severe than originally predicted, but it provides a clear if chilling example of how rapidly such infections would spread from society to society. One might argue that the scale of the issues relating to globalization appears to be too large to undertake adequate social science research. Hence, most global studies are in fact comparative and historical rather than global in orientation. Most social scientists appear to work happily with old methodologies of single-sited research.

We need new methodologies, innovative theories and almost certainly revised epistemologies to do good research on globalization processes. We do not pretend to escape from this criticism and we do not have ready-made answers to these various questions. Multi-sited, comparative and collaborative research will address some of these issues. However, it is ironic that at a time when the frontiers of methodological nationalism need a certain erasure, some social scientists are bent on reverting to a methodological parochialism under the guise of promoting indigenous social science. Most sociological theories of globalization, despite the call from C. Wright Mills and the example set by sociologists such as Immanuel Wallerstein and Charles Tilly, remain historically shallow. It is naïve to suggest, for example, that globalization started with the rise of the modern media or with the spread of American consumerism. These claims ignore the historical role of the missionary work of the world religions or the role of trade and merchant cultures since the fifteenth century or the global reach of ancient empires. Many sociologists continue to employ crude explanatory models that are typically based on some form of technological determinism such as the rise of the Internet. Understanding globalization almost certainly requires a high degree of interdisciplinary, but sociologists too frequently fail to reach outside their own disciplinary assumptions. Unsurprisingly, much of the most interesting recent work has been undertaken by human or social geographers such as David Harvey. Creative reconfigurations of the sociological discipline would be a timely step towards redesigning methods appropriate to understanding global processes Except perhaps in journalistic writings, little sociological attention is paid to Asian globalization or to the impact of Asian commodities and cultures on the modern shape of globalization. Much globalization theory is based on narrow Western assumptions, for example, that modernization and globalization inevitably produce secularization. In short, globalization is normally understood from the viewpoint of some Western issue, process or location. Little attention is paid to the impact of a Japanese aesthetic on car design or fashion or the impact of Korean film on global culture. These West-centric assumptions are still persistent despite the changing global circumstances that are consequences of the economic and political rise of China and India – two societies that account for one-third of the world's population. Tracking changes in the field of globalization studies The spatial turn Theories of globalization have been the dominant paradigm in sociology for at least two decades, but certain features of the globalization debate have been part of sociological discourse for much longer. In mainstream academic sociology, one of the earliest publications on the topic was W.E. Moore's (1966) "Global sociology: the world as a singular system". He argued that sociology was becoming a global science and that "the life of the individual anywhere is affected by events and processes everywhere" (Moore, 1966: 482). "Globalization" in this framework refers, then, to the process by which the "world becomes a single place" (Robertson, 1992), and hence the volume and depth of social interconnectedness are greatly increased. Globalization can also be seen as the compression of social space (Giddens, 1990). Geddens's definition of globalization was influenced by the so-called "spatial turn" which involved a revival of human geography which came to have a significant impact on the debate about globalization. In particular, there has been an important emphasis on the study of the global city. Globalization in this respect is treated as urban or city globalization in which a series of mega-cities (London, New York, Paris, Delhi, Tokyo and so on) became the principal sites of globalization – especially financial globalization. Cities such as London, Paris and Tokyo dominate the poli economic life of their own societies, and as a result the chief political officers of such global cities (or "lord mayors") are often dominant political figures within the national landscape. The linkages and flows between these mega-cities are thought to be more important than the linkages between states. In her major publication *The Global City: New York, London, Tokyo*, Saskia Sassen (1991, 2001) has been concerned to illustrate the mobility of capital and people within the network of such sites. These cities pose interesting political issues with respect to the national sovereignty of their own societies.

Economic and financial globalization

While it is often difficult to measure or describe social and cultural globalization, economic globalization is often relatively visible, obvious and to some extent uncontested. What is frequently debated is the actual impact of neoliberal globalization. What needs some attention, however, is the fact that neo-liberal globalization is not historically the only form of economic globalization. Social Keynesianism based on the economic ideas of J.M. Keynes, the Cambridge economist, had been a dominant but certainly contested orthodoxy in the period 1950–70. This strategy had emerged in the post-war period as a policy to improve the level of employment by directing state expenditure towards building infrastructure such as roads, railways and ports. Because Keynesianism involved major state intervention in the management and direction of the economy, it was often thought to be incompatible with liberal (and more recently neo-conservative) ideas. Towards the end of this period, economists and sociologists started to talk about the profit crisis of capitalism – falling profits, rising taxation, expanding state expenditure, declining investment, increasing strikes, high wages, and eventually stagflation. The state was now thought to be inimical to economic growth because it was assumed to impede private investment and to depress entrepreneurship. This produced new economic theories and strategies such as Reaganomics, Thatcherism and neo-liberalism, which promoted low personal taxation, rolling back the state, low corporate taxation, enterprise culture, consumer sovereignty, free trade, and the end of state subsidies. These strategies became global partly because the Cold War came to an end with the collapse of the Soviet Union in 1989–92. The collapse of communism revealed a number of societies suffering from corruption, low investment, industrial stagnation and inefficiency. With socialism in retreat, neo-liberal ideas became the dominant global orthodoxy and were often propagated by the Bretton Woods institutions as mantras for economic success. An efficient market became the main criterion of social development State socialism, despite its inefficiencies, had represented an alternative form of economic and political globalization. These communist social movements had not been given the adjective "International" for nothing. This history of global socialism (from Cuba to Vietnam and China) has been largely suppressed in the mainstream globalization literature which has concentrated on the period since the 1970s. Economic globalization has been largely seen as essentially liberal economic globalization, and hence anti-globalization movements have been largely against liberal capitalism, against free-trade orthodoxy, and against privatization and free markets. Of course, in the late twentieth century, some communist states began to liberalize their economies. In China, the Eleventh Congress of 1977, in the wake of the death of Chairman Mao in 1976, unveiled four modernization programs in four sectors – industry, agriculture, science and the military – to make China an industrial giant by the late 1980s. In modern-day Cuba and Vietnam there have been similar experiments to attract foreign capital, develop markets and diversify financial institutions such as banks. The pros and cons of this economic debate about global capitalism are difficult to assess. What is clear is that this aspect of globalization has increased inequality both within and between societies. Liberal economic globalization has also had very negative effects on the environment, increasing political conflicts over basic resources. On the other hand, the old centralist, state-dominated programs do not appear to have worked either. Towards the end of its historical centrality, the

Soviet Union became excessively corrupt and inefficient, developing an oversized and suffocating bureaucracy. The lack of political freedom, which was part of the trade-off for economic security, became unbearable in the face of ongoing economic deprivations. Bread-lines became a common sight in the Soviet Union of the 1980s. Chronic underemployment, underinvestment and industrial inefficiency and technological backwardness came to characterize these socialist societies. In addition, the powerful Soviet state had not solved its ethnic divisions and had brutally repressed its ethnic and religious minorities. With the re-establishment of the eastern Orthodox Church after the fall of communism, religious divisions and repression have resurfaced in recent years along with the growth of political authoritarianism. The collapse of the Soviet Union had been perceived by some commentators in the United States and Europe as the final victory of the liberal-democratic consensus. Francis Fukuyama's "end of history" thesis gained widespread notoriety in which he claimed that the old struggle between liberalism and socialism was over, and hence history had come to a conclusion in which liberal ideas were finally triumphant. Thus the continued unflagging and apparently unstoppable march of liberal capitalism and democracy was taken for granted. The global economic crisis of 2008–9 was a rude awakening for these champions of unfettered market capitalism and has exposed hitherto hidden forms of corporate corruption and ineptitude. Bernie Mad off in the United States was sentenced to 150 years' imprisonment for his corrupt financial practices in June 2009. The crisis in the United States and other heartlands of liberal capitalism has had significantly negative effects as far afield as Singapore, China and Vietnam, and some countries such as Iceland are now bankrupt. These catastrophic developments are inevitably raising questions about market-driven strategies and the deregulation of financial services. These economic difficulties cannot be understood within an economic framework alone, because these economic problems have multiple causes. It is thus imperative to reconsider the non-economic bases of globalization. The cultural turn In mainstream sociology, the most influential writer on the importance of religion (or more generally culture) in globalization has been Roland Robertson (1992), who has complained with some justification that social scientists had overstated the economic nature of globalization (free trade, neo-liberalism, financial deregulation, and integrated production and management systems), to the neglect of its social and cultural characteristics, especially its religious dimensions. Theories that emphasize the technological and economic causes of globalization (such as computerization of information and communication or economic and fiscal deregulation in the neo-liberal revolution of the 1970s) show little appreciation for long-term cultural, religious and social conditions. These theories of economic globalization tend to be somewhat simple versions of economic or technological determinism. Whereas Ulrich Beck (1992) and Anthony Giddens (1990) have approached globalization as an aspect of late modernity (and therefore as a feature of the risk society and reflexive modernization), Robertson has been concerned with long-term cultural developments. These include the unification of global time, the spread of the Gregorian calendar, the rise of world religions, the growth of human rights, values and institutions, and the globalization of sport. In short, we also need to attend to the various dimensions of globalization and their causal priority: such dimensions as the economic and technological (including global markets in goods, services and labour); the informational and cultural (such as global knowledge, religious revival movements and radical fundamentalism); the legal and political (human rights, legal pluralism and legal regulation of trade), and the environmental, medical and health aspects (such as pollution, ageing populations, and the market in organs and epidemics). We can simplify this discussion by suggesting that globalization has four major dimensions: economic, cultural, technological and political. Any comprehensive analysis of the future of globalization would have to consider all four dimensions and their interaction. In the 1960s Marshall McLuhan (1967) had introduced an influential vocabulary to describe the role of "the global village" in the analysis of culture and mass media in order to understand how the world was shrinking as a result of new technologies of communication. In more recent years, Castells's research on information technology and its role in shaping the world has also made a significant contribution in understanding the media in the global world. Castells's analyses touched on the globalization of information and knowledge. He also dwelt on the problems of democracy and information. The growing capacity of the Internet as knowledge provider marked a new chapter in the communication of ideas. For example, the digitalization of all library-based knowledge opens up new possibilities of a globalized knowledge society. At the same time, the issues of intellectual property rights become hugely complex. The impact of communications technology on work, as well as the growth of new types of consumerism and popular culture, is all areas of great importance in a globalized world. The globalization literature grew apace in the 1970s and 1980s.Within the sociology of religion, religious revivalism or fundamentalism was increasingly seen as a global process (Beckford and Luckmann, 1989; Robertson, 1987a). By the 1990s globalization had been identified as the "central concept" of sociology (Robertson, 1990). Religious dimensions of globalization have, however, been somewhat neglected, and most explanations focus broadly on technological and economic causes (Beyer, 1994). For example, while Ulrich Beck (2000: 53) clearly recognizes the importance of cultural globalization and "ideoscapes", his *What is Globalization?* contains no discussion of fundamentalism, Islamic radicalism, or religion in general. Sociologists have, in addition, had little to say about military globalization or about warfare. The impact of war and militarism on the origins and development of globalization has thus been neglected (Black, 1998), and yet military conflict has played a crucial part, especially with the rise of world wars, in transforming the international order into a global system. In the globalization literature, there has developed an unfortunate gap between sociological and international relations theory. Religion and military violence are therefore important but somewhat neglected causal aspects of globalization processes.

Globalization and its critics:- Social sciences are known to be windows on the present. Some fields in social sciences are too engrossed with the present to take either the past or the future seriously. In this book, because we have tried to situate the forces and processes of globalization historically, it is also incumbent on us to attempt to predict the future of globalization processes. What is the future of globalization both as a phenomenon and as an intellectual framework? Does the historical process of globalization come to an end at some point in the future? What are the chances of the world retreating into autarchic nation-states? Or is the world moving into a post-globalization phase? What would the world look like in the post-globalization phase? What kind of intellectual tools should be brought to bear to understand such hypothetical processes?

As the chapters in this study try to show, globalization theories broadly deal with the state of the affairs of the world as a whole and seek to explain the functioning of the world and its future. There are several other intellectual traditions in social sciences that also aim to understand the same processes. In examining the future of globalization, we also consider those theories that compete with the globalization paradigm. In mainstream sociology, theories of multiple modernity's may, for example, present an alternative to (monocausal) globalization theories. A number of writers on the Left have always been suspicious of globalization theories, accusing them of being simply an aspect of the neo-liberal project.

Critical theory was more inclined to advance versions of the theory of imperialism or what we might call empire studies against orthodox assumptions about liberal globalism. Others have advanced versions of dependency and world-system theories, which they believe are more adequately grounded in modern political economic realities. Yet there are other writers who bring to the study of globalization a vision of an interdependent world by invoking the ideas of Gandhi and other visionaries who refused to abandon hope in human creativity and their passion for a better world. Some of these competing theories have emerged out of anti-globalization protests or have even been proposed by the global institutions themselves. At the World Social Forum held in Mumbai in 2004 the popular slogan was: Is another world possible? The answer to this rhetorical question was affirmative. Various writers have promoted the use of an alternative terminology such as "globalization with a human face" or "just globalization" or "ethical globalization". Related expressions such as "fair trade alongside free trade", or notions such as sustainable development, more inclusive development, and democratic governance have made a fruitful contribution to public discussions. Globalization has certainly created its detractors. Now there are clearly pro-globalists and anti-globalists. These critiques of globalization have already formed the basis for a social movement against globalization in which the anti-global movement itself has become a global movement. From Porto Alegre to Mumbai, the movement has grown in strength. In subsequent chapters, we examine the origin and future of the ant globalization movements in greater detail. Some of the critical views of globalization have been translated into ideas of action and protest, especially targeted at the World Bank, the International Monetary Fund (IMF) and related institutions. Organizations such as ATTACK, a French non-governmental organization (NGO), and similar organizations have emerged in mobilizing protests against rapacious economic globalization. In two important books, *Empire* (2000) and *The Multitude* (2004), Michael Hardt, an American Left intellectual, and Antonio Negri, an Italian radical social activist and philosopher, have provided their critical assessment of the world. In the first book, they developed a theory of empire which is very different from the empires that were collections of subordinated states. In the modern empire, Multinational Corporation and other non-state organizations work together and often assume some kind of sovereignty. In

The Multitude they argue that the grip of the empire cannot last forever and that it is increasingly being challenged by the people from below with their own democratic aspirations. These masses – the multitude – seek true emancipation and can mobilize an enormous emancipator power. Here we raise two sets of questions. At the theoretical level what comes after globalization? Post-globalization, globalization, or neo-globalization, or the world of new empires? At the empirical level we must deal with the question of the fate of the earth as an ecosystem, as a place where all can live in peace, minimally defined as the absence of war and violence and an end to hunger and social insecurities in an environment of freedom. The idea of development as freedom is a powerful one and a goal that all can pursue without allowing the issue of cultural relativism to stifle debate. A minimum set of welfare provisions such as food for the hungry, shelter for the homeless and medical care for the sick must be made available and such aspirations can be satisfied within the resources of the world. Gandhi was surely right when he said that the earth has enough to meet everyone's need but not everyone's greed. In the 1970s a number of writers studied the finiteness of the resources of the earth. Their views, represented in the Club of Rome reports, identified the limitations of the ecosystem. In order to save the earth, one has to limit consumption. On the theme of the survival of humanity, *North– South: A Program for Survival* (1980), also known as the Brandt Report, and the subsequent Earth Summit report, *Our Common Future* (1987), made valuable connections between environment and development issues. Not only was the idea of sustainable development promoted, but the report also underscored the ecological interdependence among nations. The last decade of the twentieth century saw the failure of a social experiment that created the false impression and an equally ideologically charged belief that the market would solve all the problems of the world, provided the market was allowed to function without interruption, interference or distortions. Serious problems of inequality, social disorganization, violence and ecological decay marked the first decade of the twenty-first century, leading to a world-wide economic crisis. The United Nations has taken bold, visionary and often effective measures towards dealing with global poverty and various life-threatening epidemics. In the Millennium Development Goals, the UN charted a plan of action to reduce the problems of hunger and gender inequities. Regrettably little progress has been made in exercising the collective will and taking concrete actions against war and global violence. However, the UN role is limited to dispatching blue-helmeted soldiers who under the auspices of the United Nations play the role of peace keepers but not peace makers. It is now widely accepted that the global public must take a more active and collective role in stemming the tide of social dislocation and violence. The goals of a livable-in and peaceful world are not only desirable but also achievable if the public or the people have the will to make the necessary changes. True empowerment will only come from such shared knowledge and real change can only come with collective action against pollution, sex tourism and poverty. We need new values and effective institutions to combat these shared problems, and in this volume we attempt to describe some of these values as a form of "cosmopolitan virtue" in which recognition and respect for others are key components. As we write these lines in the first decade of the twenty-first century, the world is under the shadow of a growing economic crisis and is faced with mounting violence resulting from ethnic and religious intolerance. Terrorist attacks have grown out of local conditions, which have often been neglected by international agencies such as the UN, to spawn as global conditions. There is a need for renewal of certain basic, universal values such as the right to life for all. Rights to life and dignity must be cornerstones for the creation of a peaceful and compassionate world. A peaceful world must be guided by human rights and a tolerance for diversity, creating institutions to provide collective security against vulnerability. The forces of globalization must be harnessed to build solidarity and peace rather than war and destruction. An important starting point, which can itself be seen as a consequence of globalization, is to recognize our mutual vulnerability in an interconnected and interdependent world. In a world of scarcity, failure to work towards collective solutions to global problems must inevitably lead to our mutual destruction. This book will explore those themes in conjunction with the role of the global civil society and mobilization of people across cultures in charting a more comfortable future. Our expressed hope is that by reading this book, students and other readers will not only have a better understanding of the complexities - both conceptual and practical - of the world we live in but also be able to contribute to the peace that we need.

According to the World Bank (2009) press release, "Amidst global economic recession and financial-market fragility, net private capital inflows to developing countries fell to $707 billion in 2008, a sharp drop from a peak of $1.2 trillion in 2007. International capital flows are projected to fall further in 2009, to $363 billion." The UN (2009) revised its already pessimistic scenario published earlier in mid-2009, projecting that "the world economy is expected to shrink by 2.6 per cent in 2009, after an expansion of 2.1 per cent in 2008 and nearly 4 per cent per year during the period 2004–7".

References:

1. Albrow, M. (1990) 'Introduction' in M. Albrow and E. King (eds) *Globalization, Knowledge and Society*, London: Sage.
2. Althusser, L. (1977) *For Marx*, London: New Left.
3. Amin, S. (1980) *Class and Nation*, New York: Monthly Review.
4. Anderson, B. (1983) *Imagined Communities*, London: Verso.
5. Anderson, M. (1984) *Madison Avenue in Asia*, Cranbury: Associated University Press.
6. Anderson, P. (1979) *Lineages of the Absolutist State*, London: Verso.
7. Appadurai, A. (1990) 'Disjuncture and Difference in the Global Cultural Economy' in M. Featherstone (ed.) *Global Culture*, London: Sage: 295–310.
8. Archer, C. (1983) *International Organizations*, London: Allen & Unwin.
9. Archer, M. (1990) 'Theory, Culture and Post-Industrial Society' in M. Featherstone (ed.) *Global Culture*, London: Sage: 97–120.
10. Archer, M. (1991) 'Sociology for One World: Unity and Diversity', *International Sociology* 6(2): 131–47.

11. Arnason, J. (1990) 'Nationalism, Globalization and Modernity' in M. Featherstone (ed.) *Global Culture*, London: Sage: 207–36.
12. Baudrillard, J. (1988) *Selected Writings*, Stanford: Stanford University Press. Beck, U. (1992) *Risk Society*, London: Sage.
13. Beck, U., A. Giddens and S. Lash (1994) *Reflexive Modernization*, Cambridge: Polity.
14. Goldblatt, D. (1997) 'Liberal Democracy and the Globalization of Environmental Risks' in A. McGrew (ed.) *The Transformation of Democracy?*, Cambridge: Polity: 73–96.
15. Gordon, D. (1988) 'The Global Economy: New Edifice or Crumbling Foundation?', *New Left Review* 168: 24–64.
16. Waters, M. (1994) *Modern Sociological Theory*, London: Sage.
17. Waters, M. (1995) 'The Thesis of the Loss of the Perfect Market', *British Journal of Sociology* 46(3): 409–28.
18. Weber, M. (1978) *Economy and Society*, Berkeley: California University Press.
19. Weiss, L. (1998) *The Myth of the Powerless State*, Cambridge: Polity.
20. Wilkinson, B., J. Morris and N. Oliver (1992) 'Japanizing the World: the Case of Toyota' in J. Marceau (ed.) *Reworking the World*, Berlin: de Gruyter: 133–50

Chapter 2
Globalization, democracy and trade policy

Globalization poses a profound challenge to democracy. There is, however, no universal definition of globalization. Instead, globalization means different things to different people. During the last decade, globalization has become the focus of serious research as well as discussions among academics, business people, bureaucrats and politicians, but it became the focus of almost daily discussions among people of different sphere of the society as well. There is a vast literature on the subject and almost anybody has a very determined opinion about what globalization means and what kind of changes globalization will bring about. As one would expect, academics cannot agree on globalization either. For one school of thought globalization is nothing new, for another school of thought, and it seems that this one is supported by the majority; globalization is a "completely new ball game". Globalization is seen as a new engine for producing prosperity and higher income in many countries. But globalization is creating a new problem concerning income distribution within countries as well as among countries. Seen in terms of income distribution, globalization will create "winners and losers of globalization". It is very well known, that losers will fight hard to stop this process that makes them losers, whereas winners will take what they get without actively supporting globalization. This is the fundamental challenge for democracies that is being created by globalization. And because trade policy is seen as a major tool for pushing globalization, groups in societies and countries opposing globalization are also resisting a further liberalization of world trade. Instead, those groups are demanding a democratization of trade policies as well as a democratic World Trade Organization (WTO) as the major "agent" of free trade.

Three important issues of globalization will be discussed like the challenges of globalization for democracy. Secondly, to analyze the challenges of globalization and the demand for a "democratic trade policy" for international organizations like the WTO. Finally, efforts will be made to discuss scenarios and policy options for governments to respond to the challenge of globalization.......

Globalization and Localization: the Challenge for Democracy: The process of globalization is a profound challenge for democracies since it is eroding national boundaries, weakening the authority of the state and could undermine the support of the people for democratically elected governments, at least in principal.

Globalization and Democracy

Will globalization lead to the death of democracy? In today's world there are more liberal democratic countries than ever before. Especially in the 1980s and even more so after the end of the cold war in the 1990s, more and more countries moved from an undemocratic to a democratic political system. But in light of profound challenges for all democracies, some observers are afraid that the best days of democracy may already be behind us.

Localization and Democracy

There is a dilemma situation: On the one hand, there is a process of globalization going on weakening nation states and with it government's ability to care for national interests and to protect national sovereignty. On the other hand, in many democracies a process is going on that can be called localization and that means that more and more people get involved in the political decision-making process on a local level. In terms of strengthening a democratic political system, this means more direct participation of citizens and as a result a more active democracy. There is a strong incentive for politicians to listen to the people because politicians are elected and re-elected on a local level.

How to adapt democratic systems?

Globalization poses in that sense two profound challenges to democracy. First, globalization threatens democracy as such because democratic political systems are based on the territorial state and this state is being eroded by the process of globalization. Second, globalization poses a threat to the democratic political system.

Do we need a democratic WTO?

The World Trade Organization is criticized for being an undemocratic international organization, lacking transparency and deciding behind closed doors as a "rich-man's club" without broad participation. Many of those critics of the WTO demonstrated in Seattle and made Seattle a lively event and at the same time worked hard to make the WTO-conference in December of 1999 in Seattle a failure. They succeeded, but important actors inside the WTO- family are responsible for the Seattle disaster as well.

Democratic member-states or a democratic WTO?

The second problem of democratic legitimacy is the question of how to democratize international organizations like the WTO assuming that this should be done. We are not talking about international organizations with democratic countries as member-states. Taking these criteria, in most international organizations democratic countries are in the minority. That is true for the WTO, UNCTAD, World Bank and IMF.

Globalization is a challenge for all societies

Globalization is a fact of life. Globalization is, however, a double-edged sword: a powerful new engine of the world economy that raises economic growth, spreads new technology and increases living standards in rich and poor countries alike, but also an immensely controversial process that assaults national sovereignty, erodes local culture and tradition and threatens economic, social and political instability. Globalization weakens the territorial state because countries are no longer seen as distinct economic entities. Companies and financial markets, for example, increasingly disregard national borders when making production, marketing and investment decisions.

Globalization will further democracy

Secondly, governments should support democratic developments at home and abroad. In 1999, a broad coalition of states ranging in size from Cape Verde to India came together and proclaimed at a United Nations Commission on Human Rights session that all individuals have a right to democracy. .Towards a "more democratic" trade policy

Thirdly, governments should support a democratic approach to trade that must take into account the views of the developing country democracies. The industrialized democracies are still the driving force, but they are no longer a sufficient group of countries neither to tackle the old and new trade challenges nor to change the WTO to function as a more democratic institution. Developing democracies should play a "different role" in the trade decision-making process according to their volume of trade and their number and population size.

References

1. Cable, Vincent (1999): Globalization and Global Governance, London: RIIA.
2. Cerny, Philip G. (1999): Globalization and the erosion of democracy, in: European Journal of Political Research, August 1999, pp. 1-26.
3. Held, David (1991): Democracy, the Nation-State, and the Global System, in: Economy and Society, Vol.20, no.2, 1991, pp.139-172.
4. --------------(1995): Democracy and the global order. From the modern state to cosmopolitan governance, Cambridge: Polity Press.
5. Hoeckman, Bernard M. and Michel M. Kostecki (1997): The Political Economy of the World Trading System, Oxford.
6. Höffe, Otfried (1999): Demokratie im Zeitalter der Globalisierung, München: Beck.
7. Jackson, John H. (1998): The World Trade Organization. Constitution and Jurisprudence, London: RIIA.
8. Kaiser, Karl (1996): Zwischen neuer Interdependenz und altem Nationalstaat. VorschlÉge zur Re-Demokratisierung, in: Werner Weidenfeld (ed.), Demokratie am Wendepunkt: die demokratische Frage als Projekt des 21. Jahrhunderts, Berlin: Siedler 1996, pp. 311-328.
9. Krause, Joachim (1999): The Western Democracies Ü towards Prevalence or in a State of Crisis?, in: Joachim Krause, Bernhard May, Ulrich Niemann (eds.), Asia, Europe and the Challenges of Globalisation, Berlin: DGAP, pp. 187-203.
10. MacGrew, Anthony G. (1998): Demokratie ohne Grenzen? Globalisierung und die demokratische Theorie und Politik, in: Ulrich Beck (ed.), Politik der

Globalisierung, Frankfurt/Main: Suhrkamp, pp. 374-422.
11. Mathews, Jessica T. (1997) Power Shift, in: Foreign Affairs, vol. 76, no.1, 1997, pp. 50- 66.
12. Matthews, Christopher (1988), Hardball Ü How Politics is Played, New York: Harper & Row.
13. May, Bernhard (2000): Erfolglos in Seattle. Der Fehlstart der WTO-Runde, in: Internationale Politik, January 2000, pp. 49-50.
14. Mazur, Jay (2000): Labor's New Internationalism, in: Foreign Affairs, January/February 2000, pp. 79-93.
15. Ohmae, Kenichi (1990): The borderless world, London: Collins. Reinicke, Wolfgang H. (1998): Global Public Policy: Governing Without Government?, Washington, D.C.: Brookings Institute.
16. Rubin, Nancy (1999): It's Official: All of the World Is Entitled to Democracy, in: International Herald Tribune, May 18, 1999.
17. Schlesinger, Arthur Jr. (1997): Has Democracy a Future?, in: Foreign Affairs, Vol. 76, no.5, Fall 1997, pp. 2-12.
18. Zürn, Michael (1998): Regieren jenseits des Nationalstaats. Globalisierung und Denationalisierung als Chance, Frankfurt/Main: Suhrkamp.

[1]Dr. Bernhard May, Senior Fellow, Research Institute of the German Council on Foreign Relations, Berlin. He is also Secretary-General of the German Group of the Trilateral Commission, Berlin.

Chapter 3
Globalization, Conflict and the Experience of Localities

Definitions and Aspects of Globalization

Globalization is an umbrella term that refers to increasing global connectivity, integration and interdependence in the economic, social, technological, cultural, political, and ecological spheres. It is a unitary process inclusive of many such sub-processes, perhaps as best understood as enhanced economic interdependence, increased cultural influence, rapid advances of information technology, and novel governance and geopolitical challenges.

The Encyclopedia Britannica says that globalization is the "process by which the experience of everyday life ... is becoming standardized around the world." Other scholars have specifically stated that 'globalization is defined as a process through which an increasing proportion of economic, social and cultural transactions take place directly or indirectly between parties in different countries' (Radice, 3). One of the most prominent arguments against globalization has been that states held to exercise sovereignty have lost control of these processes, and therefore consequential outcomes (Evans, 201). State Sovereignty is defined in the pillars of state autonomy in the Westphalia international system. They are 'low levels of economic interdependence that do not require strong international collaborations, low information flows that limit the growth in economic interdependence, a predominance of authoritarian or non-democratic governments that limit the flow of information and people and are not morally constraint to use force against other states, and lastly, a maintenance of high degree of cultural, political, and economic heterogeneity among states that makes the coordination of policies difficult because the differences sustain a nationalist commitment to autonomy, promote varied interests and hinder communication' (Zacher, 62). The core Westphalian norm of sovereignty is no longer operative; nor can it be retrieved in the present globalizing world. There is nothing about the phenomenon of globalization that is new. One can argue that globalization has always existed; the trade between empires and their colonies could be perceived as globalization. And one can state that was the origins of its process and that today we live in an undoubted advanced stage of globalization with demolished of the bipolar world. Marxist would say that without an alternative system to challenge capitalism, capitalism is the intrinsic nature that has led to globalization. Capitalalism is a key ingredient in the dialectical process that leads to Marxism and then Communism. But with the failure of Communism in Soviet Union, we can no longer evaluate the next stage of the application of Communism. Therefore, would it be too farfetched to imply that globalization is the next natural state in the dialectical process? With no alternative system to oppose it, globalization has risen and taken a substantive stand after the collapse of USSR and no matter how we may try to distinguish ourselves from it we are part of this process. Globalization is a process whereby few institutions of our daily lives are affected. Perhaps the most notable example of globalization would be from the point of economic and industrial globalization. There is industrial globalization, which entails the emergence of worldwide production markets and broader access to a range of goods for consumers and companies. The natural outcome of the latter would be the financial aspect of globalization experienced through the emergence of worldwide financial markets and better access to external financing for corporate, national and sub national borrowers. Therefore, this creates a global economy, whereby there is a realization of a global common market, based the freedom of exchange of goods and capital. Surrounding these economic achievements and beneficiaries of a global economy, are the political structuring of wealthy nations to create a world government, which regulates the relationships among nations and guarantees the rights arising from social and economic globalization. With free trade and an evolving multinational economy, a natural discourse of cultural and social growth takes precedence. There has been an advent of new categories of consciousness and identities such as *Globalism*, which in essence, embodies cultural diffusion, the desire to consume and enjoy foreign products and ideas, adopt new technology and practices, and participate in a "world culture". Consequently, the movement of people creates transnational borders and increased immigration and multiculturalism. Although many argue that this gives birth to cultural diversity and therefore, further assimilation and acceptance of differences, others argue that this infringes on the cultural values and practices of any given culture and society. Lastly, globalization has allowed the free flow of information between geographically remote locations. With easily advanced technology, the flow of information is more rapid than in the past. Perhaps this is one of the aspects most crucial to the globalization of markets, economies and industries.

Theme in general

Given these stated definitions of globalization and a general description of what the process is comprised of, very little has been written or said about the correlation between Religion and Globalization. Given the fact most people of the world believe in a religion and/or a higher spiritual being, it is surprising that the phenomenon of globalization and its influence on Religion and vice-versa has not been further evaluated. Therefore, it is the initiative of Sociologists to discuss and clarify the effects of globalization, both positive and negative, upon Religion, its belief system and practices.

Globalization of Religion

As all major religions of the world derive from the same root source, it is importance to realize the significance of mutual respect that has been advocated in all religions. Furthermore, with globalization of free flow of information via high technology and the movement of peoples cross borders can only positively help religious tolerance to increase. This religious unity is mentioned in all religious doctrines but unfortunately, the events of history up until the present day has unfolded with the emphasis on differences than that of similarities. But if we are to revert to that which has been stated in all the following Holy verses, perhaps we can shift from religious harmony as a conception and materialize it into a reality.

The Holy Quran states:
'O Mankind, we have created you male and female, and have made you races and tribes, that you may know each other' (Al Quran 49:13).

In Judaism, it is states:
"Seek peace and pursue it.... Seek it where you are and pursue it in other places as well." (Psalm 34: 15)

In the Old Testament, it states:
"Love your enemies, bless them that curse you, do good to them that hate you, and pray for them which despitefully use you and persecute you" (Matt. 5:44)
"May God...grant you to be of the same mind with one another" (Romans 15: 5-6)
In Hinduism, Swami Vivekananda states:
"Help and not fight, assimilation and not destruction, harmony and peace and not dissension are the substance of my faith" Globalization,

History of Globalization and Religion

In discussing the issue of Globalization and its relations to religion, very little remains outside these two very significant realms of society. Religion is an institution that has existed since the emergence of the first man and humanity. On the other hand, globalization, as we perceive it today, has been an undergoing process for centuries. Although the term 'globalization' emerged as a buzzword in the 1990's after the collapse of the Soviet Union, the process of globalization had been taking place long before. In the article *Globalization since the Fourteenth Century*, globalization has been defined as "The physical expansion of the geographical domain of the global—that is, the increase in the scale and volume of global flows—and the increasing impact of global forces of all kinds on local life. Moments and forces of expansion mark the major turning points and landmarks in the history of globalization". This book then states all the factual events of history, whereby, globalization evolved when since Alexander the Great in 325 B.C., when Chandragupta Maurya becomes a Buddhist and combines the expansive powers of a world religion, trade economy, and imperial armies for the first time. Alexander the Great sues for peace with Chandragupta in 325 B.C. at Gerosia, marking the eastward link among overland routes between the Mediterranean, Persia, India and central Asia. Following this, in the first century, the expansion of Buddhism in Asia makes its first appearance in China and consolidates cultural links across the Eurasian Steppe into India, thus, establishing the foundations of the Silk Route. From the period of 650-850 A.D, there was a vast expansion of Islam from the Western Mediterranean to India; thus, this not only saw to the adoption of the religion of Islam, but all the cultural, social, and educational aspects brought about by the Islamic Civilization. An example of this would be the Ottoman Empire in 1300 AD, which spanned from Europe, North Africa, and the Middle East; this created the great imperial arch of integration that spawned a huge expansion of trade with Europe. Finally, we come to what many scholars see as the birth of Globalization; the discovery of the Americas and the travels of East and West by Columbus and De Gama. This not only inaguregated the age of European seaborne empires, but it also pioneered the exponential expansion of Christianity in these conquered regions. With the development of the slave trade in 1650, marked as a dramatic factor which sustained the expansion of

Atlantic Economy, giving birth to integrated economic/industrial systems across the Ocean—with profits accumulating in Europe during the days of mercantilism and the enlightment. The 'integration' of religions and its cultures took about a natural discourse with the merging of civilizations and their evolving trade routes, which ultimately led to the colonization of the Asia, Africa, Central and South America. Thus, here marks the pivotal point where religion becomes an integral part of globalization and vice-versa.

Present Era of Globalization

Although a brief summary of the history between the relationship of religion and globalization has been presented, the term globalization became a topic of much discussion after the collapse of the bi-polar world and Communism. Nonetheless, with recent political climax of the past several years and especially in light of the events of President Bush's war against terror and the subsequent wars in Afghanistan and Iraq, religion has been once again been evaluated from a political standpoint, whereby it has often been correlated with the effects of globalization upon it. Therefore, it is crucial to discuss and bring forth the impact of one another in a time where the two can no longer be seen as separate entities, but rather, the strong effects of globalization on religion and vice versa.

Negative Aspects of Globalization on Religion and Rcligious Ethics

Given the previous stated definitions of globalization by various scholars, it can be noted that the global dominance of globalization has affected religious and cultural values, whereby its process is seen as a threat to these traditions. For reasons such as diversity and its threat to the religious traditional values, globalization is seen as a polarization factor within these defined religious identity and its practice. The *Economic and Political Weekly* on March 27, 2004 stated the following arguments on the major interface between religion and globalization in India: (1) the major consequences of globalization have been the transmogrification of traditional religions and belief systems and (2) the beginning of the disintegration of the traditional social fabrics and shared norms by the invasion of consumerism, cyber culture, newfangled religions, social fads, and changing work ethics and work rhythms, (3) allowing people to fall back on religion for moral and social support, attributing to religion the creation and acceleration of extremist, fundamentalist, and terrorist tendencies in the third world countries, which are intended to destabilize them, and strike at the root of their civilization, and multicultural and pluralistic nature.

The book further makes an argument that globalization is the first truly world revolution. And "all revolutions disrupt the traditions and customs of a people. Indeed, they threaten a people's very security, safety, and even identity. The world revolution that is globalization in some measure threatens the security of every people on the globe". For example, with the infringement of these religious and traditional cultural values by Western Capitalists, values such as the attainment of wealth often contradicts what Islam allows as a means of wealth accumulation. This book reiterates that globalization is designed to hide and obfuscate; the form taken by imperialism in the current, increasingly worldwide capitalist system for organizing economic production and society. The inevitability of globalization and adjustment or submission of peoples all over the world to free market capitalism depends on the capacity of the dominant and ruling classes to bend people to their will and convince people that their interests are the people's interests, make them see the capitalist as their own. It also depends on the capacity of these dominant classes and their ideologues to undermine the growing resistance to the model of free market (*Economic and Political Weekly, 2004*). As the political scientist Samuel Huntington stated "money becomes evil not when it is used to buy power... economic inequalities become evil when they are translated into political inequalities." This misuse of power acquired though economic dominance has been a pattern that has increased with globalization. The monopoly of Multi-National Companies and Foreign Direct Investment of first world nations in third world nations has given them a substantial level of authority which extends from economic control to shaping political policies. This can be clearly observed in the example of the Middle East and its ongoing conflicts. The political turmoil in the whole Middle Eastern region is as much as an issue of capitalizing on the global oil market as is the issue of political and religious dispute. Although the issues of the Middle East has been primarily portrayed as one that is religious and territorial, one cannot ignore that these disputes may have been solved long ago if the policies of that region were not shaped and affected by nations who control the oil cartel, which is so crucial to the survival of many first world nations. So as argued before, globalization and religion cannot be seen as separate entities, but rather, they are intertwined in a way that influences the course of political and economic discourse. Using examples from Bangladesh, even though statistics show that Bangladesh is underdeveloped, there are sufficient features in the developments works both in public and private sectors which will expose that the rich are reaping the benefits whilst the under privileged remain at the bottom of the socio-economic stratum. The consumer market economy does not in any way indicate any concern for welfare of the poor in particular. On the contrary, the economy assumes that the poor will get their share of development and benefits along the normal course of development. This is a true exposition of a laissez- faire economy, where profit making gets priority over welfare and ethics. This is where there is a direct contradiction between Islam and capitalism/consumerism. Even though a country such as Bangladesh does gain from the process of globalization, when compared to wealthier nations, there lies a stark contrast. Furthermore, with the advancement of technology and its means of media and the free flow of information, terror groups have used their political agendas by using religion as a tool to fulfill these political gains. Simultaneously, the same source of media and information has been successful to portray this global misconception of Islam or Muslims as extremists or terrorists. Perhaps the larger issue at hand is not religion per se, but the growing disparities of the rich and the poor, between classes and between developing and first world nations. These economic, political and cultural disparities that are the growing repercussions of globalization often are misconstrued as a fundamentalist religious cause.

Positive Aspects of Globalization on Religion

Thus far, the negative repercussions and complexities of globalization and its infringement on religion and culture and its attribution to class differences have been presented. That is not to say that globalization is all negative. It has also brought about a culture of pluralism, which is so prevalent in all religious teachings. With globalization, we have seen the emergence of global human rights and environmentalist groups that protect the interests of those often victimized by globalization. Furthermore, with the creation of Organizations such as the United Nation, World Health Organization and World Bank, etc., whether effective or not, has increased means of transparency and security. In this regard, the creation of a peaceful 'global village' has allowed the issues of poverty, war, and environment to have a global consensus and participation. This integration has allowed the erosion of cultural, ethnic and religious differences that often pertained as ideologies that divided in the past. Therefore, with the free movement of populations and the immigration, we have seen the development of multiculturalism and perhaps mutual understanding and respect.

The Holy Quran declares:
"We have sent three Inspiration to Ibrahim (Abraham), Ismail (Ishmael), Ishaq (Issac), Ya'qub (Jacob) and the Tribes, to Isa (Jesus), Ayyub (Job), Yunus (Jonah), Harun (Aaron) and Solaiman (Soloman), and to Dawud (David) we gave Psalms. Of some messengers we have already told thee the story……s

(Surah Al Nisa 4: Verse 163-164).

Essentially, all religions teach these shared principles of love, patience, peace, justice and equality. The Unity of the Creator and mankind are the essence of all religions as sent trough the Holy Prophets and messengers of God; from the first Man and Prophet, Adam (AH), to successive Prophets such as Prophets Noah (AH), Abraham (AH), David (AH), Moses (AH), Jesus (AH), and Prophet Mohammad (SAW), (Peace Be Upon Them), there has been a call for human understanding and peace. They have all carried the messages of God to bring forth a perfect equilibrium towards our existence on earth. They have shown us the way to achieve this harmony in the institutions of Marriage, Society, Education, Politics, Justice System, Economics/Trade and all the other remaining spheres of our lives.

An Islamic View

Islam not only recognizes all the Messengers but also makes no discrimination between them. The Holy Quran says:
"The Messenger Mohammad (SAW) believes in what has been sent down to him from his Lord and so do the believers. Each one believes in: (a) Allah, (b) His Angels, (c) His Books and (d) His Messengers. They say we make no distinction between one and another of His Messengers. We hear and obey, oh! Lord and seek your forgiveness"
(Surah Baqara 2 vs.285).

Referring to the honorary status bestowed upon Prophet Ibrahim (Abraham) (AH) as a Friend of our Lord it is mentioned in the Holy Quran: *"And who can be better in religion than one who submits his face (Himself) to Allah; and he is a Muhsin (a Doer of good). And follows the religion of Abraham the Hanif (Monotheist). And Allah did take Abraham as a Khalil (an intimate friend)."* (Sura Al –Nisa: vs125).

As the descendants of Prophet Ibrahim (AH), prophets of our Creator, Prophet Musa (AH), and Prophet Mohammad (SAW) share the religion and teachings of their ancestor, Prophet Ibrahim (AH). Given this fact, it is only appropriate all religions collectively seek inter religious cooperation through dialogue to further seek knowledge on the prayers that were asked by the holy Prophets. The Holy Quran repeatedly declares that the high status and dignity must be given to these Prophets as an essence of Islam, which reveals the acceptability of other Prophets. In the era in which the term globalization has been given concrete definitions by which most of the world and its diverse religions, cultures, languages are an integral part of its process, it is crucial that we look upon something that is more definite to unify us in a positive direction, By utilizing the free flow of communication easily available through advanced technology, religions should focus more on the humanitarian and pluralistic aspects of their teachings as a means to lessen the divide. Furthermore, religion understanding can be one of the most essential means by which foundations of peace and harmony can be achieved. By overlooking differences and uniting under the doctrines of our Creator, we can oversee that the functioning of global groups ad their strive towards humanitarian equality is not just rhetoric but a reality. Whereas the adoption of economic aspect of globalization overrules those of the spiritual needs of humanity, let religion be the principles by which we follow to fill the vacuum of inequality that is so often created by globalization of capitalist economies and free markets. The integrated economic, social, and political needs are subordinate to imperatives of faith and morality. Faith as a whole should be seen as a collective unity of all religions, so that they may emancipate themselves from the negative consequences of globalization. As stated in the Holy Quran and so eloquently practiced by Prophet Mohammad (SAW) in his roles as a spiritual guide, a head of state and leader of community, a supreme judge and arbitrator of dispute, a reformer of society; that we all descend from the religion of Prophet Abraham (AH) and we all look upon our Creator as the ultimate source of perfection and emancipation.

The source of religion is not to divide but to unite to bring upon this justice and equality in this world, whatever the challenges and adversaries may be.

Proposed Recommendations

"When a society devotes resources to education and training, when it encourages individuals to believe that their life chances will be significantly related to their accomplishments, and when it provides an attractive array of choices, that is good reason to believe that individuals will be moved develop some portion of their innate capabilities. Thus, it may be argued, equality of opportunity is the principle of task allocation most conducive to the crucial element of human good". –

William Galston In order to foresee a world that gives precedence, respect and equal status to all religions, their ethics and practices, a more collaborative application of modified policies of States and Global Organizations must be taken. Furthermore, the repercussions of globalizations on these specific cultures can be minimized with alternative state and global strategies. The following are a number of suggested policies that should be adapted in order to lessen the disadvantages created by globalization on religion and religious groups.

(1) All States of the world cannot politically discriminate any Religion. In the example of Bangladesh, its Government recognizes all religions and religious holidays. All States should comply with this policy.
(2) Heads of States should prioritize their political agendas by reiterating the importance of religious unity in examples made in state functions' by quoting from different religions on the importance of religious understanding, mutual respect and emphasize on the unity of religion to bring about peace and justice.

(3) Every Religion preaches Peace as the foremost importance; therefore, Religious groups and religious leaders must work to disseminate this.
(4) All Economic and Regional Forums such as ASEAN, SAARC, EU etc. must strive to bring about an economic stability by taking initiatives to balance foreign exchange.
(5) There should be a balance of trade, whereby smaller countries can benefit from subsidized rates given to them by more economically powerful nations.
(6) The negative repercussions of political globalization can be prevented once more powerful nations cease to impose and interfere in the smaller nations' political discourse. Rather, powerful nations should aid to establish democratic systems. Additionally, neighboring nations should facilitate these countries.
(7) A worldwide theme of poverty elimination should be implemented. Examples of Dr. Yunus's micro-finance projects that have been successful in Bangladesh can be adapted.
(8) Alternatively, and more importantly, from an Islamic point of view, the implementation of *Zakat* (charity) system in Islam, whereby, 2.5% of wealth be distributed to the poor or poor other poor countries is the key to alleviate the poverty.
(9) Organizations such as the United Nations should increase transparency and accountability by eliminating the process of Veto Powers given to a few selected economically and politically powerful nations. This will give these nations less dominance on the global political and economic arena and its discourses and outcomes.

Chapter 4
Globalization and Child Labor

There is no empirical evidence that globalization increases child labor. If anything, globalization reduces child labor. In a country that starts out with a largely uneducated workforce, globalization raises the wage rate of uneducated, relative to educated workers. Unless the government takes steps to counter the reduction in the incentive to educate children, the net effect of globalization is likely to be an increase in child labor. By contrast, in developing countries that has spent sufficiently for education to have a relative large number of workers with at least a basic education, globalization raises the wage rate of educated, relative to uneducated workers. In these countries, public intervention is needed not to raise the incentive for parents to educate their children, but to loosen liquidity constraints. Developing countries can turn globalization into an opportunity to reduce child labor by spending more on education and public health. Developed countries can help them by financing these policies, compensating them for short-term adverse effects, and stopping agricultural protectionism.

General viewpoint

Economists have long been aware that international trade is beneficial on efficiency grounds, but has strong re-distributive implications. The "Corn Laws", that depopulated the countryside in 18th Century England, and created the pre-conditions for the industrial revolution, are a prime example of what can happen when barriers to trade come down. A prime example of what can happen if barriers stay up is provided by the European Common Market's agricultural policy (CAP), part of the political deal that permitted the West European integration to be set motion after the end of World War II. By keeping internal farm prices systematically above world levels, and dumping excess production on to the world markets, the CAP, and similar policies carried out by North American countries, contributed to the transformation of subsistence farmers in industrial workers (and shanty town dwellers) throughout the developing world (Boserup 1981, Chapter 15). The question here is, given that there may be gainers and losers from globalization, are children likely to be among the former, or among the latter? More specifically, is further trade liberalization and industrial integration on a world scale likely to raise the number of children engaged in work activities? If the answer is yes, and given that globalization is unlikely to stop (because many gain from it), what can be done to remove such a consequence? Section 2 examines the available evidence. Sections 3 and 4 interpret it in the light of household economics and trade theory. Section 5 discusses the policy implications.

Does globalization increase child labor?

Globalization is the process by which an increasing share of world production is traded internationally, and the productive systems of different countries become increasingly interdependent. It started soon after the end of the second world conflict, but gathered momentum in the 1980s, as rapid progress in information technology compounded the effects of falling transport costs and trade liberalization (Krugman, 1995). It thus seems reasonable, in trying to understand the consequences of globalization, to look at what has happened over the last couple of decades. Most of the existing analyses are concerned with the effects of globalization on wages and employment in the developed world. Since our concern is child labor, and child labor is concentrated mainly in the developing world,1 we focus on the experience of developing countries. A useful source of information is the World Bank's *Development Indicators.* Using these, and subsidiary information provided by Sachs and Warner (1995), we constructed a World Panel, consisting of the data available on each developing country for the years 1980, 1990, 1995 and 1998. Since economic structure and 1 though not on a comparable scale, child labor is becoming a problem also in developed countries. There, however, it is largely connected with clandestine immigration (an example is the illegal importation of Chinese children to work in the Italian leather industry and rag trade). One way or another, the main source of child workers is thus the developing world.

Economic policies differ substantially between Africa, Asia and Latin America, we shall look at each continental area separately, as well as at the developing world as a whole. The measure of child labor that figures in the *Development Indicators* is the participation rate of individuals aged 10 to 14. The limitation of this measure is that it does not count children working at younger ages (the participation rate for the age group 6-10 is far from negligible)2, and children engaged in unofficial, especially if illegal, work activities. It thus leaves out what are probably the most undesirable forms of child work. In addition to this measure of child labor, we thus consider the primary school non-attendance rate (the complement to unity of the primary net enrolment rate reported in the *Development Indicators*). The problem with using the latter as an indicator of child labor is that children not attending school are not necessarily working (in the home or elsewhere).3 However, since children not attending school are more difficult to monitor by the authorities than children who do, and thus more exposed to the worst forms of abuse (from hazardous or very hard work, to soldiering and prostitution),4 the non-attendance rate is at least a danger signal. Poverty is generally assumed to be the main cause of child labor. Indeed, as it has been observed there is a negative association between income and child labor. For similar levels of per-capita income, however, both our indicators of child labor show very large variations. That may be partly due to the fact that countries with similar levels of per-capita income can have very different income distributions, but partly also to the effects of different policies. In a sample of Indian rural households, Cigno and Rosati (2000) find that the characteristics of children reported by their parents as neither working nor attending school are very similar to those of children reported as working full time.

Globalization and child labor: harnessing globalization for children: *a report to UNICEF*

For all their limitations, these indicators give us a broad-brush picture of the evolution of child labor over time, and across countries. Higher primary enrolment is associated with lower labor participation among the 10-14 year olds. The correlation is far from perfect, however, not only because the primary enrolment rate refers to a younger age group than the 10-14 child participation rate, and because work in informal or illegal labor markets is likely to be underreported, but also because a sizeable proportion of both age groups combines, in some countries, work with school attendance. What about globalization? Is there a direct link between exposure to international trade and child labor? To measure a country's relative position in the globalization process, we use the standard measure of trade openness: the sum of imports and exports, expressed as a percentage of GDP. Later, we shall also use the classification of trade openness in Sachs and Warner (1995). According to this very stringent criterion, a country may be called open if it has *none* of the following characteristics:

1. Non-tariff trade barrier covering 40 per cent or more of trade
2. Average tariff rates of 40 per cent or more
3. A black market exchange rate that is depreciated by 20 per cent or more relative to the official exchange rate, on average, during the 1970's or the 1980's.
4. A socialist economic system
5. A state monopoly on major exports. As evidences show, exposure to international trade does not appear to encourage child labor. On the contrary, higher foreign trade appears to be

associated with a lower incidence of child labor. Here again, however, we find considerable national differences. At low levels of trade, countries similar in terms of exposure to trade can be very different in terms of child labor incidence. A clearly negative association between trade openness and child labor is evident only for Africa and Latin America. In Asia, the relationship between trade and child labor is much weaker (especially if the latter is measured as a complement to the school enrolment rate). This seems to indicate that the type of activity in which a country specializes, and the policies it pursues, shift the relationship between child labor and globalization. There is, therefore, no *prima facie* evidence that globalization will necessarily result in more child labor. Indeed, there are signs that international trade and economic integration offer governments the opportunity to *reduce* child labor. Since trade promotes economic growth, the opportunity could come in the form of higher income. Or it could be that the relative wage changes brought about by international trade are conducive to less child labor. Let us try to understand how.

Why do children work?

The first thing to be kept in mind, in answering this question, is that children do not normally *choose* to work. Most have that decision taken for them by their parents. Even in the case of the child who was expelled or run away from home 6, the reasons for his or her present working can be traced back to parental actions that made it impossible for the child to remain in the home. The only real exception are children who were abducted, and children who lost, or were separated from, their family of origin because of war, or of some natural disaster (Cigno, Rosati and Tzannatos, 2001). Parental actions affect the number of working children under their control in three ways. By conditioning the probability that a child is born. By conditioning the probability that the child will survive to an age, as early as when he or she can be made to work. By actually making the child work. On all three accounts, household It makes little practical difference whether the child jumped or was pushed. Economics is the appropriate conceptual framework within which to examine the emergence of child labor. An assumption often made in the household economics literature is that parents8 act as a kind of benevolent dictator as in Becker (1981). Except in extreme cases, however, many of the behavioral implications are the same if it assumed that parents are ultimately self-interested as in Cigno (1993) and Rosati (1996). So long as parents care about their own, as well as their children's consumption, the decision whether to send a child to work or to school does in fact depend on essentially three things: the cost (including the opportunity-cost) of education, the expected return to education, and the extent to which parents are able to finance educational investments. Conceptually, parental decisions may be described as a two-stage process. Parents decide whether to procure the birth of a child, and how much to spend for the child's health and nutrition, under conditions of uncertainty about whether the child will survive to school age. The probability that the child will survive is conditioned not only by external causes, but also by how much the parents spend for the child. If the child survives, parents decide how the child's time should be allocated between work and study. They also decide how much of the family budget (augmented, if the child is sent to work, by his or her earnings) is spent on the child. If the child is sent to school, parents also decide how that sum is to be divided between consumption and educational expenditures. Stage 2 of the decision process can have one of three possible types of outcome. One occurs if the marginal cost of human capital (say, the cost of increasing the child's future earning capacity by one dollar) is higher than the maximum that parents are willing to pay. If that is the case, the child is made to work full time. Another arises if the marginal cost of human capital is lower than the minimum, at or below which parents are willing to buy as much education as possible. If that is the case, the child does not work at all. Between these two extremes, there is a third possible type of solution, where the child works and attends school at the same time. Parents, in that case, allocate family income, and the child's own time, to the child's education up to the point where the marginal cost of human capital just equals the price that parents are subjectively willing to pay for it. An important role is played by the capital market and educational policy. Suppose that, by acquiring education, a child could substantially enhance his or her future earnings. If they could borrow against those future earnings, parents could finance the child's education and current consumption, and leave also something for everyone else. If that is not possible, however, the child's education and current consumption would have to be financed out of the parents (and other members of the family's) See Becker (1981), Cigno (1991). Whether it is the father, the mother or the two jointly who make the decisions, and how the balance of power is affected by external events, is important from several points of view, but not particularly relevant in the present context. The cost includes not only the actual expenditure for books, transport, etc. incurred sending the child to school, but also the opportunity-cost (forgone income) of keeping the child away from work. The willingness to pay for this cost reflects the expected return. This liquidity constraint establishes a direct link between current income and child labor participation: only families with above subsistence income can contemplate investing in a child's education. Educational policies such as free schooling or subsidized educational material can help relax the constraint, but not eliminate it. To eliminate it altogether, there would have to be scholarships generous enough to cover the child's current consumption, and on a large enough scale to reach all liquidity-constrained families. Capital market imperfections thus help explain the finding of a negative effect of income on child labor at the aggregate level: as GDP rises, the proportion of liquidity-constrained families falls, and the extent to which a government is able to finance educational policies (if it so wishes) rises. Now take as step back, to the first decision stage. Since the child's survival probability is conditioned not only by external causes, but also by the actions (parental expenditure for the child's nutrition and health) taken by the parents themselves, the latter face a trade-off between procuring an extra birth, and improving the survival chances of the children that they already have. In taking their first-stage decisions, parents take into account not only this, but also the other trade-off, between work and education, that they will face at the next decision stage (if the child lives that long). The external causes that condition the probability of a child's survival include not only climate and genetic factors, but also government expenditure on sanitation, and public health. The higher this expenditure, the higher, other things being equal, the probability that a child will survive to school age, an later to adulthood; the higher, consequently, the return to investing in that child's education. If public health expenditure is a complement for private expenditure on the child's health and nutrition, an increase in the former will induce parents to raise the latter; if it is a substitute, the effect may be the opposite (Cigno, 1996). An increase in public health expenditure could thus induce parents to have fewer children, and spend more for each of them, first on health and nutrition, then on health, nutrition and education. Under standard assumptions, household economic theory makes a number of important predictions about the effects of changes in the economic environment. A lump-sum increase in household income (*e.g.*, a government subsidy) tends to reduce the proportion of school-age children that works. It also tends to raise the amount spent by parents for the health and nutrition of each child, and for the education of each child that attends school. These effect are stronger if parents have difficulty in borrowing, because the increase in current income relaxes the liquidity constraint. The effect of income on fertility is ambiguous, because it raises the expected marginal utility, but also the expected marginal cost of children. The effect on the *absolute* that raises an additional problem. If the motive for investing in children is non-altruistic (but also for equity towards other members of the family), parents will be reluctant to allocate family resources to a child's education, unless the child's enhanced future earnings will in some way benefit the parents themselves (or the family as a whole); *cf.* Cigno (1993), Rosati (1996). Expenditures on nutrition and health reduce not only mortality, but also morbidity. Since the two are positively correlated, everything we say about the effects of parental and government actions on the probability premature death applies also to the probability of illness (and thus to a child' future ability to work or study with profit). We talk of mortality for short, but most of the time we mean "mortality and morbidity". In Becker's terminology, public health expenditure could thus trigger a substitution of quality for quantity (of children). For a detailed exposition, see Cigno, Rosati and Tzannatos (2001). number of children who work is also ambiguous, because the *proportion* of school age children that works falls, but the number of school-age children may increase (either through an increase in fertility, or through a reduction in infant mortality large enough to more than compensate for the fall in fertility). If the income change is the product of an increase in someone's wage rate, and of a change in someone's labor supply in response to the wage rate increase, there will be substitution as well as income effects, and the signs and sizes of both will be different depending on *whose* wage rate has increased. Suppose that the wage rate for *unskilled* labor rises. This means that not only unskilled adult workers, but also child workers, are paid more per unit of time. As the opportunity-cost of time spent in education will consequently go up, the marginal cost of education. will rise. At the same time, as the remuneration gap between educated and uneducated labor will become smaller, the return to education will fall. Both these changes will reduce the incentive for parents to invest in their children's education. If the income-effect is not large enough to compensate for the substitution effect, an increase in the unskilled wage rate will then raise child labor. Evidence related to the farm productivity child labor in India suggests that this may indeed be the case (Cigno and Rosati, 2000). By contrast, an increase in the remuneration of *skilled*, or just literate, adult workers would raise the return to education, and thus the incentive for parents to produce fewer, better educated children. In households where the parents themselves are skilled workers, or if parents are able to borrow against their children's expected future earnings, the substitution-effect will be reinforced by the income-effect. That makes it likely that a skilled wage rate increase would reduce not only the number of children, but also the labor force participation of each school-age child. Wage rate increases encourage also the labor participation of women with children. This introduces yet another effect on child labor. In the short run, a wage increase will tend to raise the number of working children, as young girls will be called upon to substitute for their mothers in the performance of domestic chores; in particular, looking after younger siblings (Basu, 1993). As the opportunity-cost of their time increases, however, women will be less willing to give birth to more children (Cigno, 1991). In the long run, the supply of potential child workers could thus fall. Public expenditure on health, sanitation, etc., induces parents to have fewer children, and to spend more for each child, if private and public expenditure are complements; the other way round if they are substitutes. Evidence consistent with the hypothesis of complementarily is reported in Cigno and Pinal (2001), Cigno and Rosati (2000), Rosenzweig and Wolpin (1982). If that is the case, an increase in public health expenditure will reduce child labour. If capital market imperfections make it difficult for parents to discount the future benefits of educational investments, the reduction in the demand for children is merely a reflection of the fact that a child who goes to school costs more to his parents than one who works. If parents can discount their children's future earnings, the reduction in the demand for children comes from the fact that a smaller number of educated children can have the same total expected income as a larger number of uneducated ones. Also public expenditure on education induces parents to have fewer children, and to spend more for each child, and is thus likely to reduce child labor. Survey evidence that school enrollment responds positively, and child labor negatively, to various indicators of public school provision is reported in Cigno and Rosati (2000), Ravallion and Wodon, (2000), Ray (2000), Rosati (2000), Rosati and Tzannatos, 2000).

The effect of trade

Why do countries trade? The answer, handed down by Ricardo, is comparative advantage. A country can increase its welfare if, instead of directly producing all the goods its members wish to consume, it specializes in the production of those goods that it can produce at relatively lower cost than other countries, and exchanges the surplus for the goods it does not produce. What determines this comparative advantage? Since the cost of a good depends on the prices of the factors used for its production, and the prices of traded inputs are the same everywhere, differences in the relative costs of traded goods reflect differences in the relative prices of non-traded goods used as factors of production. In turn, the relative prices of these immobile factors reflect differences in factor endowments. Standard (Heckscher-Ohlin) trade theory predicts that countries specialize in the production of traded goods that make more intensive use of the non-traded factors of which they have relatively greater abundance. In traditional classroom accounts of Heckscher-Ohlin theory, the non-traded factors are labor and capital. Countries with a relative abundance of labor (developing countries, the so-called South) will thus export labor-intensive products, countries with a relative abundance of capital (developed countries, the so-called North) will export capital-intensive products. Since, within each country, an increase in trade raises the price of the abundant factor relative to that of the scarce one, an implication of this vision of the world is that "globalization" will make workers worse-off relative to capitalists in the North (hence the alarm of trade unions), better-off in the South (then why the opposition of so many self-appointed paladins of the underprivileged?). This vision of the world has somewhat changed over the last couple of decades. Partly, this reflects a general re-thinking of the development process. While early growth theory equated economic growth with the accumulation of physical capital (buildings and machinery) per head of population, modern theory does in fact attach much greater importance to the accumulation of human capital (knowledge and personal skills). Partly, however, the change of emphasis comes also from a recognition that physical capital is not immobile. Machinery can be moved around, and buildings can be taken down and rebuilt anywhere. All that is needed is the financial capital (equity or debt instruments) to pay for plants and machinery. Since financial capital is highly mobile, physical capital is then mobile too. Human capital is embodied in skilled workers. These are more mobile than unskilled workers, but they, too, have their international mobility restricted by immigration rules and sentimental ties. As a broad generalization, one might then say that the fixed factors determining the comparative advantages of different a countries are their different endowments of labor skills. Of course, in the same way as capital endowments can be modified by investment, so skill endowments can be modified by education. But education takes much longer than the purchase of a new machine, or the construction of a plant, and workers are by and large more durable than physical capital. Starting from this premise, Adrian Wood has re-formulated the theory of comparative advantage in terms of relative skill scarcities: countries export the products which make greater use of the relatively more abundant type of labor. Within each trading country, the benefit of increased world trade will then accrue to members of the relatively larger skill group. For most purposes, the relevant skill categorization is into illiterate (including workers with an incomplete primary education), literate (those with just a basic education) and skilled (those with a higher level of education, or a marketable skill in addition to basic education). In developed countries, where there are comparatively more skilled than literate workers, and the number of illiterates is insignificant, globalization widens the gap between skilled and unskilled wage rates. By contrast, in developing countries with a relative abundance of literate workers, what widens is the wage gap between literate and illiterate workers; the wage gap between skilled and just literate workers becomes narrower. In developing countries with relatively more illiterates, the wage gap between this and other categories of workers will narrow. There is ample evidence of increasing wage dispersion, and of a consequent increase in income inequality in developed countries (Krugman, 1995; Krugman and Venables, 1995). The inability to explain this phenomenon by means of the traditional trade theory prompted the re-interpretation of Heckscher-Ohlin that we have just mentioned as well as other theoretical developments to which we shall refer later. Evidence on developing countries is sparser, but it, too, appears to support the predictions of reconstructed trade theory. As shown in Wood (1994), there is a negative correlation between changes in income inequality, as measured by the Gini coefficient, and changes in the income share of manufactured exports to developed countries. Since the exporting countries have all got relatively more unskilled (literate or illiterate) workers than the countries to which the exports go, evidence that inequality and exports tend to move in opposite directions is consistent with the hypothesis that comparative advantages reflect relative skill endowments. This has important implications for child labor. By definition, working children fall in fact in the "illiterate workers" category. By and large, these children belong, or originate from, poor rural families. Their parents are more likely to be illiterate than literate, and very unlikely to be skilled. In developing countries with comparatively more literate than illiterate workers, trade then leads to an increase in the gap between literate and illiterate wage rates. As pointed out in the earlier section , that gives parents an incentive to produce fewer, better educated children. If parents cannot borrow against their children's future earnings, however, educational investments are subject to liquidity constraints, and these constraints are all the more stringent in families where the parents are illiterate (*i.e.,* 18 Cigno and Rosati (2000), Rosati (2000), Rosati and Tzannatos (2000). precisely in those families where children are more at risk of being put to work). As already pointed out, there could also be a short-run increase in the number of young girls working in the home, as their mothers are induced to seek outside employment. In developing countries with comparatively more illiterate than literate workers, trade reduces the ratio of literate to illiterate wage rates. Here, the argument is the exact opposite of the one used for countries with a relatively large literate population. On the one hand, the incentive for parents to have fewer, better educated children is reduced. On the other, poorer families become less poor, and this may tend to reduce the number of working children, though not by much. The net result is likely to be a rise in the number of working children. In a developing country, trade expansion *could* thus help reduce child labor. Whether it actually does depends to a large extent on education. In countries that start out with too few educated people, parents will see their incentive to produce more educated people reduced, rather than increased. The opposite is true of countries that start out with enough educated people to give them a comparative advantage in exporting goods with a high content of this type of labor, but the greater incentive to produce better educated children will translate into actual school enrollments only to the extent that poorer families, where child labor is mainly concentrated, can afford the investment. Income re-distribution would thus help reduce child labor, but simulation experiments suggest that it would have to be carried out on an unrealistically large scale to have any noticeable effect (Cigno, Rosati and Tzannatos, 2001). Public school provision, educational subsidies, and generous maintenance scholarships ar more effective. As adult female labor participation increases in response to rising female wage rates, gender-specific educational policies may be required to counter a possible short-run tendency by female children to substitute for their mothers in the performance of domestic work. As explained in the last section, public health expenditure, which directly and possibly indirectly reduces mortality, and thus increases the incentive to make human capital investments, also would help. All of this is consistent with the cross-country evidence reported in further discussion..

Intra-industry trade

Globalization does not simply mean more international trade for final goods. It also means more trade in intermediate goods. Falling transport costs and advances in information technology facilitating the coordination of dispersed production activities, are in fact favoring the segmentation of production processes, and the location of different segments of the same process in different countries. Although much of the resulting intra-industry trade is among developed industrial countries, the potential of These parents are poor to start with. They become poorer if trade lowers their wage rate in absolute terms. The opposite would be true only if the illiterate wage rate, while falling relative to the literate wage rate, increased in absolute terms. The income-effect is ambiguous, because it tends to raise the number of school-age children, and to reduce their labor participation. The relaxation of the liquidity constraint, associated with higher earnings, tends to do the opposite. implications for developing countries, and thus for child labor, cannot be lightly dismissed. The growing literature on this new aspect of international trade emphasizes the effects of market size on the international division of labor. Duranton (1998) adds an extra dimension to the debate by pointing out that, since the output of different segments of the same production process must be ultimately combined into a final good, the extent to which these different segments can be carried out in different countries is limited by the ability of different work forces to produce intermediate goods that will prove mutually compatible. As this means, in large measure, ability to deliver goods in time, and of the right quality, satisfying the compatibility requirement is clearly facilitated by the existence of work forces with similar characteristics. That is consistent with the observation that intra-industry trade has so far occurred mainly among countries at the same stage of development. This argument points to a trade-off between comparative advantage (which privileges *trade with unequal's*) and compatibility (that favors *trade with equals*). Tension between the two considerations may lead to complex dynamics, with a phase in which international trade is driven primarily by differences in relative factor endowments, and one in which work forces with similar characteristics form integrated production systems (coalitions of individuals, who are better off trading with one another, than with the world at large) that will uncouple from the rest of the world economy. The danger of this for the developing countries is that, instead of increasing wage inequalities *within* countries, which provide the stimulus for educational investment, international trade could end up increasing inequalities *between* countries (Krugman and Venables, 1995). The emergence of clubs of developed countries who speak only to one another is associated with the availability of educated workers in sufficient numbers to make it possible to create integrated productive systems spanning more than one country. Developing countries with a largely uneducated workforce thus face a double risk: that exposure to international trade may reduce the incentive for their inhabitants to educate their children, but also that they may be excluded from trade and economic integration with the richer countries That reinforces the conclusion reached in the last section about the importance of accompanying exposure to international trade with vigorous educational and health policies, capable of rapidly increasing the proportion of educated workers in the country's total labor force.

Cross-country evidence

We have seen that exposure to international competition *may* result in more children going to school, rather than to work. We have also seen that a necessary condition for this to happen is that a country opening itself to international competition should have a sufficiently large share of educated workers. We have seen, finally, that policies aimed at lowering mortality are likely to also reduce child labor. To test these propositions, we must measure the effect of trade on child labor while holding all the other variables (income, health expenditure, skill composition of the labor force) constant. Using the data in our

Global Panel, we regressed child labor on trade openness, real per-capita income, health policy, and skill composition. It would have been desirable to control also for differences in income distribution, but our data are not sufficiently consistent across countries and dates of observation to permit that. Child labor is alternatively measured by the 10-14 labor participation rate, or by the primary school non-attendance rate. Trade openness is alternatively represented by the trade ratio (exports plus imports, divided by GDP) or by a dummy taking value one if the country is open according to the Sachs-Warner definition, zero otherwise. Real per-capita income is measured as GDP (in constant PPP terms) per head of total population. Health policy is represented by the share of public health expenditure in GDP. Skill composition is represented by the share of the 15-65 workforce which completed primary education only, and by that which attained secondary or higher education (the share of those who did not even complete primary education is used as the reference group). Descriptive statistics are reported . Skill composition captures essentially the cumulated effects of past educational policies. In view of the fact that current educational policies may affect the incentive to send children to school, it would have been desirable to measure the effects of these policies on child labor. Since child labor is a close correlate of school attendance, however, there was no way we could do that with our data. reports fixed-effects, OLS estimates, over all developing countries, of the relationship between the conventional measure of trade and our two alternative measures of child labor. If skill composition is not controlled for, trade *raises* the 10- 14 labor participation rate, but has no significant effect on the primary school nonattendance rate. Income and public health expenditure reduce both measures of child labor. If skill composition is controlled for, trade has no significant effect on either measure of child labor. The effects of the skill composition have the expected signs. The proportion of workers with completed primary education has a negative effect on child labor, and so does that of workers with secondary or higher education. If the dependent variable is the

10-14 labor participation rate, however, the share of workers with secondary or higher education reduces the significance of the workers with completed primary education. Conversely, if the dependent variable is the primary school non-attendance rate, what is non-significant is the share of workers with secondary or higher education. The picture is somewhat more favorable to globalization if the trade ratio is replaced by the Sachs-Warner measure of openness. Openness reduces child labor, however measured, even if we do not control for skill composition. The share of workers with primary education is non-significant if the dependent variable is the 10- 14 labor participation rate, while that of workers with secondary or higher education is non-significant if the dependent variable is the primary school non-attendance rate. These findings are consistent with the theoretical considerations of the last section. What the data tell us in essence are that, other things being equal, international Its complement if child labor is measured by the primary school non-attendance rate! To allow for unobserved heterogeneity across countries and dates of observation. Competition reduces or, at worst, has no significant effect on child labor. Interestingly, the more optimistic scenario is associated with the more stringent definition of trade openness, the one that takes into account the conditions under which trade takes place, rather than the actual volume of trade. Since the beneficial effects of international exposure come through relative price changes, it is in fact not irrelevant whether internal prices are subject to government control, or free to adjust to international prices, and whether foreign trade is distorted by quotas and state monopoly or not. The estimated coefficients of the skill composition variables measure the effects of increasing the proportion of educated (or of more highly educated) workers, holding all the other variables, openness included, constant at their mean values. Given that openness is quite high on average (43.4 percent of the sample is "open" by the Sachs-Warner definition, trade is on average a third of GDP), these findings are compatible with the theoretical proposition that (a) trade increases the skill premium in countries with a comparatively more educated workforce, and (b) only countries with a sufficiently educated workforce are able to integrate in the emerging global economy. The share of public health expenditure in GDP significantly reduces the 10-14 labor participation rate whether or not we control for skill composition. But its effect on the primary school non-attendance rate is insignificant if skill composition is controlled for. This finding is coherent with the theoretical arguments and micro-econometric evidence mentioned in above, namely that health and educational outcomes are jointly determined by health and education policies. This may indicate that skill composition is correlated with current educational policies. The picture does not change a great deal if we consider the three continents separately. The only notable difference is that, in Africa and Latin America, the effect of the trade ratio is significantly negative even when skill composition is not controlled for. Since the effect of trade openness also is significantly negative everywhere, this strengthens our conclusions about the beneficial effects of international integration *per se*. In Africa, the effects of the share of the workforce with only primary education are never significant. Given the comparatively small size of this group of workers in that continent, that seems to confirm our considerations regarding the risks of globalization for countries that start out with a largely uneducated workforce.

The effect of agricultural protectionism

A notable feature of the growth of international trade since World War II is that the share of agricultural goods in the total exports of developing to developed countries has fallen from nearly a quarter in 1955, to barely a fifth in 1989. Over the same period, agricultural exports from developed to developing countries have staid roughly constant at just under a fifth of the total. That may be judged positively, from the viewpoint of developing countries, if one believes that industry is where technical progress occurs, and that industrialization at any cost is thus the only key to development. A closer look at what many developing countries export, however, reveals that much of the growth in manufactured exports consists of low-tech goods, made internationally competitive by the low wage rates prevailing in the exporting countries. By contrast, the Green Revolution experience, and agricultural productivity growth in developed countries, suggests that developing countries with a high ratio of cultivable land to population may have forgone the opportunity of exploiting their comparative advantages, for no great benefit in terms of productivity growth. However one judges it, this is in some measure a consequence of agricultural protectionism in Western Europe and North America. As mentioned in the Introduction, the European Common Market (now Union), the United States and Canada have tended to shelter their own farmers behind tariff barriers and import quotas, and to further distort international competition by directly subsidizing them. Hong-Kong, Singapore and Taiwan, with their very low ratios of land to people, are a different story.

The resulting agricultural surpluses have been sold below cost, or donated in times of food crises, to developing countries. This policy has discouraged agricultural production in developing countries. By holding food prices, and thus wages, low in developing countries, it has also made it easier for these countries to produce and export manufactures with a high content of unskilled labor. Ending agricultural protectionism would bring efficiency gains. It would also cause a re-distribution from European and North American farmers, to European and North American consumers, and to Third World farmers. Since child labor is predominantly supplied by farming families, or by former farming families who have immigrated to the cities, in the developing world, the welfare of working children would undoubtedly rise. Under certain conditions, child labor would fall. We have seen that simply making parents richer has ambiguous effects on child labor. To be sure that child labor will fall; the return to education has to rise. That would happen spontaneously in the longer term, as increased international demand for agricultural imports, and the higher quality standards required by first world markets, induce farmers in developing countries to adopt modern production methods. That can in fact be expected to put a premium on skilled, or at least literate, labor. The process could be accelerated by deliberate policy, by spending on education and health on the one hand, and encouraging technical development in agriculture on the other. There is empirical evidence of an enhanced effect of educational policies on school enrolment in parts of India that had been touched by the Green Revolution (Lavy, 1985; Behrman, Foster, Rosenzweig and Vashishtha, 1999).

Conclusion

There is no empirical evidence that globalization increases the incidence of child labor. If anything, the available cross-country evidence shows that globalization can reduce child labor. There is evidence also that educational and health policies affect child labor. The theoretical explanation may be summarized as follows. The parental decision to make a school-age child work depends on the costs and benefits of education. Due to capital market imperfections, parental investments in their children's education are limited by liquidity constraints. Wage rate changes affect both the costs and the benefits of education, and the liquidity constraint. Exposure to trade raises the wage rate of the comparatively larger skill group, relative to that of the others. In a country that starts out with a largely uneducated workforce, globalization raises the wage rate of uneducated, relative to educated workers. The cost of education, that includes the opportunity-cost of time spent in education, will then rise relative to the benefit, that reflects the wage differential between educated and uneducated workers. This will reduce the incentive to educate a child, and raise the incentive to have more children. On the other hand, the wage change may relax the liquidity constraint on the poorest families (if the wage rate of uneducated workers, children included, increases in absolute terms).

These surpluses have tended to become smaller in recent years, thanks to reduced farm subsidies in North America, and production quotas in the European Union. Incentive to educate children, the net effect of globalization is likely to be an increase in child labor. Indeed, according to some variants of new trade theory, these countries are at risk of uncoupling from the more developed countries, as the latter form exclusive clubs that trade only with one another. In a country that starts out with a relatively large educated workforce, globalization raises the wage rate of educated, relative to that of uneducated workers. If we distinguish between basic education, and higher (or basic plus technical) education, can then expect the wage rate of the higher educational category to rise relative to that of the lower category in developed countries. By contrast, the wage rate of the lower educational category can be expected to rise relative to that of uneducated workers in developing countries that spent sufficiently for education in the past, to have a relative large number of workers with a basic education. In this elite of developing countries, the benefit of education will rise relative to the cost, thereby making it more advantageous to have fewer, better educated children. On the other hand, the wage change may tighten the liquidity constraint on the poorest families (those with uneducated parents, if the uneducated wage rate falls in absolute as well as relative terms), where most child workers originate. Here, therefore, public intervention is need not to raise the incentive to educate a child, but to help parents overcome the liquidity constraint. What can a developing country do to help itself, and turn globalization into an opportunity to reduce child labor? The policies recommended include, obviously, school provision, educational subsidies, and maintenance grants for school children. They also include public health expenditure, which raises the incentive to make educational investments on a child, and helps to reduce fertility. What can develop countries can do to help developing countries to participate successfully in the globalization process? First, they can help developing countries finance their educational and health policies. For countries with a largely uneducated workforce, temporary shelter from international competition is probably unavoidable until a sufficiently large proportion of workers is educated at least to primary level. More generally, these countries need to be compensated for the adverse short-term effects of changes in productive structure. Second, developed countries can stop protecting their own farmers. By allowing globalization to extend to agriculture, the countries of West Europe and North America would help stem the internal migration from the country to the cities of the developing world, which is a major cause of urban child labor, and the exportation of child labor to the developed world.

References

1. Basu, A.M. (1993), "Family Size and Child Welfare in an Urban Slum" in C.B. Lloyd (ed.) *Fertility, Family Size and Structure,* Population Council, New York
2. Becker, G. (1981), *A Treatise on the Family,* Harvard University Press, Cambridge, Mass.
3. Behrman, J.R., Foster, A.D., Rosenzweig, M.R. and P. Vashishtha (1999), "Women's Schooling, Home Teaching, and Economic Growth", *Journal of Political Economy* 107, pp. 682-714
4. Boserup, E. (1981), *Population and Technology,* Basil Blackwell, Oxford Cigno, A. (1991), *Economics of the Family.* Clarendon Press and Oxford University Press, Oxford and New York
5. Cigno, A. (1993), "Intergenerational Transfers without Altruism: Family, Market and State", *European Journal of Political Economy* 7, pp. 505-518
6. Cigno, A. (1998), "Fertility Decisions when Infant Survival is Endogenous", *Journal of Population Economics* 11, pp.21-28
7. Cigno, A. and C. Pinal (2001), "Endogenous Child Mortality, Price of Child-Specific Goods and Fertility Decisions: Evidence from Argentina" in D. Heymann, F.

Navajas and E. Bour (eds.) *Latin American Economies*, Macmillan, London (forth.)

8. Cigno, A. and F.C. Rosati (2000), *Why do Indian Children Work, and is it Bad for Them?*, IZA DP N° 115, Bonn
9. Cigno, A., Rosati, F.C. and Z. Tzannatos (2001), *Handbook of Child Labor*, The World Bank , Washington D.C. (forth.)
10. Duranton, G. (1998), *Globalisation, Productive Systems and Inequalities*, Centre for Economic Performance, London
11. Grootaert, C. and R. Kanbur (1995), "Child Labor: An Economic Perspective", *International Labor Review* 134, pp. 187-203
12. Krugman, P. (1995), "Growing World Trade: Causes and Consequences", *Brookings Papers on Economic Activity* 1, 327-377
13. Krugman, P. and A. Venables (1995), "Globalisation and the Inequality of Nations", *Quarterly Journal of Economics* 110, 857-880
14. Lavy, V. (1985), "Cropping Patterns, Mechanization, Child Labor and Fertility behaviour" *Economic Development and Cultural Change* 33, pp. 777-791
15. Lavy, V. (1996), "School Supply Constraints and Children's Educational Outcomes in Rural Ghana", *Journal of Development Economics* 51, pp. 291-314
16. HARNESSING GLOBALISATION FOR CHILDREN: *A report to UNICEF*
17. Ottaviano, G. and D. Puga (1997), *Agglomeration in the Global Economy: A Survey of the New Economic Geography*, CEPR WP N° 1699
18. Ravallion, M. and Q. Wodon (2000), "Does Child Labor Displace Schooling: Evidence from Behavioral Responses to an Enrollment Subsidy", *Economic Journal* 110, pp. 158-176
19. Ray, R. (2000), "Analysis of Child Labour in Peru and Pakistan: a Comparative Study", *Journal of Population Economics* 13, pp. 3-20

20. Rosati, F.C. (1996), "Social Security in a Non-Altruistic Model with Uncertainty and Endogenous Fertility", *Journal of Public Economics* 60, pp. 283-294
21. Rosati, F.C. (2000), *Morocco: Reducing Child Labor by Increasing School Availability.* World Bank WP, Washington DC
22. Rosati, F.C. and Z. Tzannatos (2000), *Child Labor in Vietnam: An Economic Analysis,* World Bank WP, Washington DC
23. Rosenzweig. M.R. and K.J. Wolpin (1982), "Governmental Interventions and Household Behavior in a Developing Country", *Journal of Development Economics* 10, pp. 209-225
24. Sachs , J.D. and Warner, A. (1995) "Economic Reform and the Process of Global Integration", *Brooking Papers on Economic Activity* 1
25. Wood, Adrian (1994), *North-South Trade, Employment and Inequality,* Clarendon Press, Oxford

Chapter 5
Rural women and globalization

The participants of the Expert Group Meeting examined the situation of rural women in the context of globalization. The discussion indicated that globalization involves changes in a wide range of areas, including:

- trade liberalization;
- greater mobility of capital and increased financial flows;
- changes in labor demand and restructuring of labour markets (flexibilization2);
- changes in the process of production;
- changes in the role and function of the state;
- rapid diffusion of products and consumption patterns;
- faster diffusion of information and technology;
- new forms of governance and mechanisms of regulation;
- Emergence of "global civil society".

The participants agreed that these processes of globalization are articulated within existing local contexts and mediated through local power constellations, existing gender relations, class and ethnic divisions as well as regional disparities. The impact of globalization should be considered in terms of short-term and long-term gains and losses for women. It was also recognized that the effects of globalization are not gender-neutral. Taking into account the above factors, the Meeting focused on the following political and economic aspects of globalization affecting the rural sector:

- commercialization of agriculture;
- transition to market economy;
- further integration into the global market;
- labor- intensive industrialization;
- emergence of global commodity chains (GCCs);

- shift to high value food and cash crops;
- expansion of agribusiness industries;
- rapid change in agricultural technologies;
- wider use of information and communication technologies;
- privatization of resources (such as land and livestock) and social services (health, education);
- labor migration;
- structural adjustment policy involving cuts in public spending.

These aspects, which will be further elaborated in the following section, provide the context within which the situation of rural women was examined. It should be noted that the Flexibilization of labor markets can be defined as a reduction of stable, permanent work and an increase in temporary and flexible work. distinction between rural and urban sectors becomes blurred as production and labor markets get increasingly intertwined. During the discussions it became clear that the following more general trends affecting rural women's livelihoods could be identified:

- The changing nature of specialization brought about by globalization entails that certain economic activities become more attractive and others less so; the effects of these changes on rural women are mediated by gender, ethnicity, race and class.
- The long-term prospects for men and women who have been displaced due to market integration may differ. This will depend on their human resource endowments and physical assets, as well as socio-cultural norms which have a bearing on the gender division of labor.
- Women's traditional reproductive role may restrict them from seizing new opportunities created by globalization. When women do take up new opportunities they may experience tension between their productive and reproductive roles.
- Socio-cultural norms are constantly undergoing change. In some ways processes of globalization are

accelerating such transformations through the changes in employment and income earning opportunities and diffusion of consumption patterns, lifestyles, the media, new technologies and products.

In general, the participants agreed that rural women encounter new opportunities as well as experience additional limitations and negative impacts due to the changes. In the short run, it is possible that some livelihoods of rural women may be threatened due to the changes in the organization of production. It was agreed that in order to reduce the vulnerability of rural women in the short run, there is a need for developing an appropriate support system to assist them in their survival strategies. In the long run, in order to achieve and sustain the benefits that may be associated with globalization, it is necessary to design interventions to secure their livelihoods in this competitive environment by way of improving their access to resources and enhancing their human capital. Moreover, it is necessary to engage in social activism aimed at changing the existing norms that shape the gender division of labor.

The following sub-section discusses the changing socio-economic and political environment within which globalization is taking place and the next sub-section provides framework for analyzing the situation of rural women within the context of globalization.

1. Changing socio-economic and political environment

The rural sector in many countries is diverse, ranging from well developed commercial large-scale and medium-size farms to family operated, small land holdings which may be devoted to subsistence production and/or market production.

As agricultural and livestock production is becoming more intensified and population pressures increase, some of these small land holdings are becoming increasingly marginalized and are actually producing at the sub-subsistence level.

The changes that are occurring in agricultural (crop, horticulture, live stock) production as well as in aquaculture and industry are key elements for understanding how global changes are affecting and influencing women's lives. In many cases, there has been an increase in employment opportunities for women, especially wage employment in agro industry (especially fruit, vegetables and flowers), rural industry and export-oriented industries, including export processing zones (EPZs), as well as more self-employment (e.g. trade, handicrafts, food processing). These positive developments, however, have not been enjoyed fully due to the fact that many women lack the necessary resources and safety nets to enable them to maximize their benefits. At the same time, traditional forms of income and subsistence are eroding in many countries. As women are often reliant on these livelihood sources, their erosion may affect them negatively. The meeting identified five dimensions of the changing environment. These are: the role of the state; commercialization of agriculture, labor intensive industrialization and export processing zones (EPZs); changing labor markets and nature of work; and new information and communication technologies (ICTs).

a) **The role of the state**:- Globalization is compelling states to alter their relations with the market and civil society, as such; states are mediators of change. In many countries the onset for this changing role was the structural adjustment policies, which entailed significant cutbacks in public spending and the provision of basic services. For transition countries the dual political and economic transformation has led to a considerable decrease in public provisions and services as well. It is now increasingly recognized that the state has a critical role to play in the provision of basic services, particularly to rural areas where there may not be clear incentives for the private sector. States are important actors in providing a conditioning, and often enabling, environment for the market economy, including commercial agriculture. As a consequence, a variety in the way production is organized depends in part on their policy choices. These policy choices have important implications in terms of creating enabling conditions (or not) for small farmers and making rural areas and livelihoods more appealing.

b) Commercialization of agriculture. The forces of globalization have brought about far reaching changes in the pattern of specialization within agriculture. In many areas, subsistence agriculture is giving way to commercialized agriculture, in which both small and large farmers are involved in the production for the market, and increasingly for export markets. Other forces such as rising income and urbanization have already been creating conditions conducive to the commercialization of agriculture. But globalization has added momentum to this process by liberalizing trade regimes and by allowing freer movement of capital.

An important consequence of producing for the export market in the context of freer mobility of capital is the growing involvement of giant agro-business complexes in developing country agriculture. This has the potential of radically transforming the agriculture sector of developing countries, leading to the industrialization of agriculture that has already taken place in the developed parts of the world. At this stage, however, this phenomenon accounts for a relatively small proportion of commercialized agriculture in the developing world. Many people, including rural women, are engaged in smallholder commercial agriculture. However, the industrialization of agriculture is leading to erosion of the "classical international division of labor" in agricultural production in some countries. The so-called nontraditional agricultural export commodities or high value foods (HVF) are becoming relatively more important than the traditional exports of coffee, tea, sugar and cocoa. These new HVF include fruit and vegetables, poultry, dairy products and shellfish. . The success of these so-called New Agricultural Countries (NACs) in pursuing their HVF strategy has depended on a combination of factors, including favorable international market conditions during the early phase, dominance and availability of domestic and foreign capital, high degree of concentration in the industry (especially in production, processing and marketing) and reliable supply of inputs. Two characteristics seem to determine the competitiveness of HVF sectors. One is the pursuit of low cost production, primarily obtained through low labor costs, in particular that of rural women. Second, HVF competitiveness depends on reaching a high degree of quality, which is important for establishing a presence in niche markets. The role of consumers in OECD countries as well as increasing standards of food safety and quality requirements (phyto-sanitary regulations) are important elements in the functioning of agro-food system. The agro-food industry is also characterized by the emergence of GCCs. The emergence of these GCCs has been significantly aided by new technologies in transportation and the computerization of much of the production process ranging from drip -irrigation to packing and increased specialization in livestock production. As a result of these trends, producers of traditional export commodities may see their market position erode as may smallholder family farmers.

An important facet of the global integration of agricultural markets is the organization of production through "contract farming" with rural producers. This means that the exporters or food giants control the production of commodities through providing technical assistance, finance, and controlling the use of fertilizers and pesticides, as well as types of seeds planted. The contract farming system can provide the opportunity to obtain an income from land-based production, to adopt improved production methods and a link to the market. Yet rural producers can also face risks of exploitation by middlemen and fluctuation in prices. With the exception of a few globally operating food giants, transnational corporations

(TNCs) tend to adapt their strategies to local conditions under which HVF and more traditional commodities are produced. Depending on local circumstances there may be some differences in the degree of control giving more or less flexibility to local farmers.. It was also recognized that under certain circumstances, traditional processes are gaining new dimensions. A case in point is the nomadic pastoralism in Mongolia, where the recent privatization of livestock and increased market integration pressured herders to adopt more commercialized activities such as producing cashmere for a growing international economic niche market. About 24 low and middle-income countries were responsible for more than US$500 million HVF exports by 1990. Most of these countries are located in Latin America and Asia. See: Watts, Michael. J. and David Goodman. 1997. "Agrarian Questions: Global Appetite, Local Metabolism: Nature, Culture, and Industry in Fin-de-Siècle Agro-Food Systems." In, David Goodman and Michael J. Watts, (eds), 1997. *"Globalizing Food: Agrarian Questions and Global Restructuring"*. London: Routledge: 1-34.

Labor-intensive industrialization and export processing zones (EPZs). With the changes in the organization of production there has been an increase in labor-intensive, often export - oriented, industries located in developing countries as well as in transition economies. This development has important implications for rural areas as it entails their further integration into the market. This market integration involves a wide variety of activities ranging from rural industries to the establishment of EPZs. Rural industrialization includes independent entrepreneurs producing for the local market as well as sub-contracting for larger domestic and foreign firms. Examples of rural industrialization are textiles and garments, food processing, carpet weaving and toys. Government policies, including those that are favoring the establishing of EPZs, are aimed to attract foreign capital by providing special arrangements such as tax breaks and suspension of environmental and labor laws. The economic incentives provided by governments made labor-intensive industries more attractive, and for the firms establishing themselves in the EPZs women became the preferred labor force because given the level of skills required, female labor was found to be cheaper than male labor. However, as has been well-documented, the valuation of women's "skills" formed part of a process of gender stereotyping which depicted women as docile, nimble-fingered and only working for some pocket money, as they were not seen as the breadwinners.

Changing labor markets and nature of work:- The "flexibilization" of work and labor market liberalization are among the defining characteristics of the economic environment in the era of globalization. These changes have been accompanied by labor-market deregulation. As a result, in some sectors regular, full-time employment is being replaced by more diverse patterns of employment such as irregular part-time employment, outsourcing, home-based work and other forms of temporary labor arrangements which escape standard labor legislation. Such changes in the labor markets are decreasing the relative tax burden of business and making production responsive to increased volatility in demand, while shifting the costs of economic adjustment and change onto the most vulnerable, usually women. Within this process, employing female labor became more attractive because they can be hired for low pay and under less than desirable working conditions in comparison with men. With some exception, the majority of women, especially in developing countries are filling the irregular, low paying jobs with little training or promotion prospects. Although the gender differential affects of the employment and displacement of the labor markets under globalization are still controversial and not always predictable, the share of women workers particularly in the labor intensive sectors has, so far, been quite high. In the context of globalization, more and more poor rural women are able to find temporary and, in some cases, more permanent jobs in large-scale enterprises driven by export cash crop farming; agro-processing plants; and export -oriented industries, including export processing zones. Trade in natural medicinal resources, operations of agency communications systems and home-based piecework such as leather tanning, packaging and labeling are other work opportunities that have become available to some rural women with the changing work environment. For the vast majority of the rural poor – women, children and men – sporadic construction work in the cities, informal trading and trucking are some of the more conventional activities that offer opportunities to supplement household earnings..Despite the diversification of job opportunities, much of the work that rural women are able to engage in are either at the margins of emerging industries, where high turnover rate of labor is common, or in the informal sector. The increased choice and opportunity women are finding in the labor market may have a short life and gender inequalities may be intensified in the long run. Furthermore, although women are becoming more economically active in paid employment, they still remain economically disempowered with weak bargaining power and lower incomes. In addition, increased women's participation in paid work has not diminished women's responsibilities for household tasks and childcare. The burden of unpaid work at home and a marginal position in the labor market tend to reinforce each other, making it harder for women to break out of the role of dependent and secondary breadwinner within the family. New information and communication technologies (ICTs) within the context of globalization ICTs constitute an important interface in the transfer of resources as well as in the organization of production. The global trend is to move toward knowledge driven society (the network society) mediated by ICTs. ICTs have the potential to break the isolation of rural women and improve their access to education and training. ICT-based education will not only be important for capacity-building of rural women and girls, but may also assist in providing more food security as rural women and girls may gain better knowledge about markets and prices. If effective measures are not taken urgently, it is highly probable that an ICT divide could widen urban-rural disparities in education and access to new forms of knowledge. This could create great disadvantages to rural households in structuring their livelihood strategies. As rural women and girls run significant risks of being further marginalized in the knowledge society and economy, it is important to specifically target them for programmes and training. . *Framework for analyzing the situation of rural women in the context of globalization* An essential feature of a globalizing economy is the shifting division of labor associated with changes in the nature of specialization and production processes. How these changes affect rural women depend in the first instance on two proximate factors: what role women play in the declining activities and how equipped they are to take advantage of the expanding activities. These two proximate factors depend in turn on a large number of underlying forces operating at the individual, household, community, state and global levels. For instance, individual skills and command over resources would have a bearing on the extent to which women participate in declining as well as expanding activities. Household structure and the nature of intra-household division of labor (1999 World Survey on the Role of Women in Development, Globalization, Gender and Work, United Nations, New York, 1999, p.) will also affect women's opportunities and their ability to take them. Furthermore, their ability to seize the new opportunities and to fend off the new threats will also depend upon social norms impinging on gender division of labor in the broader economy, and the extent to which women can play an effective role in decision-making processes at the household as well as community levels. However, these underlying forces are not immutable. The constellation of these forces is constantly being altered by the processes of globalization itself, interacting with other changes occurring in the spheres of economic policy, demography, technology, and socio-cultural values.

In order to understand the situation of rural women in the context of globalization, it is therefore essential to first note women's existing conditions with regard to their command over skills and resources, household structure and gendered division of labor, and women's role in decision-making processes, and then to examine how the processes of globalization are affecting all of them. This report undertakes such an analysis and structures the analysis in the following manner. The report identifies two major channels through which the effects of globalization are being mediated, namely changes in livelihood patterns and changes in the patterns of labor mobility. The next section undertakes a discussion of rural women's livelihood patterns, how they are changing in the wake of globalization, and what effects they are having on the well-being of women in terms of their access to resources, income-earning opportunities and working conditions. The following section looks at the changing patterns of labor mobility and analyses how these changes are affecting the opportunities open to women. In light of the discussion presented in these two sections, the report then goes on, in the next section, to trace the changes that are taking place in the underlying factors such as household structure, household division of labor and gender relations that have a bearing on women's well-being.

B. Diversification of livelihood:-

With increased market integration most rural households are not able to support themselves exclusively on land based activities. Therefore, the majority of households have diversified their sources of livelihood either as a survival or an accumulation strategy. This was made possible by re-structuring household division of labor to enable households to maintain their status as independent family cultivators while at the same time engage in the non-farm and non-rural sectors. The strategy a household can adopt depends on, among other factors, access to productive resources such as land, capital, education and skills. In part, this strategy can influence how households allocate their labor between farm and non-farm sectors and between wage and non-wage labor. Under market conditions the main bottleneck rural households face is cash availability. Therefore, those households with diverse sources of livelihood and predictable and regular cash earnings are able to achieve the highest level of security. Availability of cash enables households to hire labour and also invest in non-farm activities. The relatively better off farmers are able to maximize their cash earnings by venturing into non-farm activities such as operating a small grocery store, restaurant, and café in the village or nearby town centre or taking up a regular wage/salary job in the private or public sector. Supplementing land based earnings with a stable and regular non-farm income enables such households to maximize their survival and creates the possibility of savings and, for some, the accumulation of capital. The women and children of such households often do not have to work outside the home. On the other hand, households that are at the lower end of the social strata have little or no resources at their disposal to diversify their sources of livelihood. These households, whether they may have access to land or not, often must rely on cash or in kind earning of family labor for their subsistence. The situation of rural women within the context of globalization, particularly those at the lower end of the social strata, varies according to their access to resources and employment opportunities. Access to resources and benefits even within the context of diversification most households in rural areas still depend on land and natural resources for their basic subsistence. Rights of control over land are important, since they determine access to other factors, such as, extension services, credit and membership to farmers' organizations. In some countries, rural women continue to be deprived of equal rights to land by law. In other countries, although they may have de jure rights, they do not have de facto rights. In some cases, customary rights to land and other natural resources often enabled women to engage in and benefit from agricultural, livestock and forest based production. However, the privatization process, notwithstanding some exceptions, which has accelerated the process of land titling, land consolidation and reorganization of the use of common property is increasingly undermining property rights, thus, depriving women of direct access to land. Privatization tends to lead to the concentration of property rights (such as access, use, control) distributed within the household and the community into the hands of male household heads or local elites. Some non-farm activities of rural women depend on access to a natural resource base. Intensive production and harvesting of forests for global markets have accelerated the degradation of critical natural resources on which the rural women from poor households depend for livelihood to augment their income. Rural women are closely associated with local ecological resources and manage biodiversity on a daily basis. A renewed interest in bio-diversity and indigenous plants and materials has created opportunities for rural women to utilize their traditional knowledge and experience to take advantage of emerging national and global markets. However, these possibilities may not be realized unless Trade Related Aspects of Intellectual Property Rights (TRIPS) are implemented in a transparent and just manner to protect the rights of local communities to indigenous resources. An important issue is the possible effects of increased privatization of agriculture extension services and financial markets on rural women whose access to information and credit is already minimal. Rural women's access to agricultural support systems has traditionally been limited, not only because extension workers generally worked with male heads of the households, but also due to the time constraints faced by women to participate in such programmes due to their heavy work load. Privatization of agricultural extension services will further adversely affect the prospects of women's access to these services. Agriculture being a high-risk venture, credit to farmers is not easily forthcoming in many countries, particularly to women. Furthermore, the cyclic nature of production and thus income creates unique constraints to access credit from commercial banks. Though many countries followed the practice of providing agricultural credit under concessional terms, the current changes directed to develop competitive credit markets could pose problems to farmers in their access to capital, unless the private sector steps in to fill the capital gap. Any changes resulting in reduced access to capital for rural households have implications for production investment and thus their livelihood strategies. Provision of micro- finance is a popular measure to support rural women's access to income generating ventures. The impact of micro-finance initiatives for rural women in general is rated to be positive. But differences are evident among the micro-finance programmes in demonstrated approaches, commitment and success related to capacity building among rural women to be self-reliant producers and confidant credit holders in their individual rights. As liberalization and financial market integration accelerate, with focus on competitive credit and efficient financial management principles, the concern would be to provide a sustainable access to micro-credit for rural women. Additionally, it should be recognized that micro-credit for petty trade should be only the entry point for economic advancement of rural women, but long-term focus should be upgrading their economic enterprises to ensure sustainable livelihood.

New employment opportunities and working conditions:- Commercialization of agriculture together with trade liberalization, especially in developing countries, have created new employment opportunities for women in rural areas which are also accompanied by new risks. For instance, export crop expansion may force women from permanent agricultural employment into seasonal employment. In Thailand for example, women started to subcontract to multinational corporations on family-owned plots to produce baby corn and asparagus on former paddy land or started to raise shrimps under contract to foreign companies. Often such employment arrangements in the agricultural export sector entail low pay labor- intensive manual jobs. However, despite its low wages, the net returns from such activities may be an improvement over the traditional agricultural activities it is replacing. Such is the case in Thailand, where women now earn more in a shorter work day than what they did by cultivating rice. Globalization is affecting the livelihood prospects of rural women not only through its effects on agriculture but also through its effects on industry. Trade liberalization coupled with free movement of capital has enabled many developing countries to set up export industries using cheap labor. This has opened up employment opportunities for women, especially in the garments and electronics sectors. In many countries in South and Southeast Asia, women are moving in large numbers from rural to urban areas to make use of these opportunities, resulting in a distinct feminization of labor force in export-oriented industries. In most cases, previously these women did not have any job prospects at all. The most they could aspire to was the life as a maid, or a prostitute, or a petty trader. For them, the prospect of employment in export industries has amounted to improvement in their livelihood opportunities, with far-reaching economic and social consequences (see for example, Tzannatos 1995)6. Livestock production in developing countries is also undergoing major transformation due to global demand for variety of livestock products particularly from developed countries. These demands are diversifying livestock production, and are also creating new industries around livestock products similar to what is happening in the agricultural sector. While the changes in the organization of livestock production may favour male labour, female labor appears to be preferred for the labor intensive tasks involved in the processing and production of livestock products. New technologies for agricultural production are leading to the creation of new employment opportunities in rural industries and agribusiness enterprises. However, such opportunities may favor those who have certain skills, capacities and access to social networks and assets. This may pose a danger for women unless they are provided with education and training to acquire the necessary skills. Such a selective phenomenon is evident where employers in certain export industries prefer young women with some education over older women who often do not. This problem becomes acute when the nature of specialization shifts from relatively unskilled activities to skill intensive activities. On the other hand, withdrawal of state provisions for basic services often increases the burden of reproductive work on women thereby restricting their ability to take up opportunities in productive, paid employment.

In general rural women work long hours, and under difficult circumstances often without proper technologies to ease their productive and reproductive work. The wage levels are still lower for women compared to men. In some organized sectors, the new jobs entail low wages and poor work conditions and the unorganized agricultural and informal sectors are totally outside of the sphere of formal labor laws. In addition, new work arrangements have also been introduced to increase the competitiveness of agribusiness enterprise, rural industries or export processing zone firms and contract farming. Such arrangements may involve complex contractual arrangements which are not self-evident to the poorly informed new employees who have low or no formal education. Nevertheless, women in rural areas and especially those who are under extreme economic deprivation seem to prefer the option of having access to jobs with pay irrespective of the terms. In this connection, domestic work, in the cities or abroad, has for long been a major source of employment for the poor women of rural areas. For instance, many Filipino women migrate to become nannies or housekeepers. The intensification of trade in services, over the past two decades has increased and broadened the scope for such work for women in many parts of the developing world. By and large, the benefits accruing to rural women and men, through new economic opportunities brought by globalization differ due to prevailing gender norms and inequalities. Men appear to be reluctant to assume work traditionally associated with women (particularly reproductive work) unless there is an increase in status or when it is well paid. Women may be reluctant to assume work traditionally associated with men, but do so out of need.

C. Changing patterns of labor mobility:-

The demand for cheap labor in the newly emerging industries, agribusinesses, EPZs and services that were established often with the help of foreign capital continues to be strong. Women are preferred workers because they can be hired for lower pay in "irregular" jobs and often under less favorable terms than men, and easily dispensed when their labor is no longer needed. This process is particularly important in view of the ongoing process of impoverishment in rural areas due to diverse factors such as land scarcity, over-grazing, a loss of productive and monetary value of land and a decrease in agricultural productivity. Daily hardship, and lack of educational and social services continue to be strong push factors. In some cases, rural women (and men) leave their villages to take advantage of employment opportunities elsewhere, including overseas. Migration has, thus, become both a process and consequence of globalization. Movements of labor have been from rural to rural, as young women and men join the work force of agribusiness; rural to urban, where girls and adult women leave for towns and cities to enter the service and manufacturing sectors, including the EPZs; as well as internationally, to work as nannies, maids, factory workers, entertainers, or teachers and nurses. In some instances, the migration is cyclical or temporary, in others, it is more permanent. In most cases, labor movement is voluntary. However, there has also been a rise in forced migration, such as the trafficking in women and girls for sex work, domestic service, or sweatshops. There are many actors involved in the migration process. States, private enterprises and market forces influence the structuring and channeling of migratory flows. At the household level the whole family or household may be involved in the decision which family member should be migrating. At times middlemen or agencies play a central role in organizing the migration of rural people, with possible risk of exploitation, in particular for women and girls. Although generally migration results in the redistribution of tasks and responsibilities among those left behind, there appears to be a strong difference as to the impact of migration on household division of labor and gender relations depending on whether a woman or a man is migrating. When migration results in the loss of male labour, households resort to different strategies in order to survive. One strategy, in the social cultural setting in which women are able to enter male domains, is for the women to undertake the work previously done by migrants.

Sometimes, however, this strategy may result in the work not being done. The absence of a husband or other male head of household often forces women to take over his tasks and responsibilities. While this means increasing women's burden, it may have empowering effects as this affords a woman the opportunity to acquire new skills (e.g. negotiating with government departments and traders, learning to use agricultural equipment). Women may (e.g. in Egypt) also experience an upward occupational mobility due to vacancies, which under different circumstances would have been occupied by men. Another strategy, when migrant remittances are sufficient, is for women to utilize this income to contract labor for certain agricultural and livestock production tasks traditionally done by men. In addition, when remittance income permits, some women are able to hire labor to assume some of the most labor-intensive tasks, allowing them to assume income-generating activities off farm. However, in some societies a man's role and responsibility may be taken over by a male relative, or the woman whose husband migrates has to move in with her husband's relatives. In these instances the women cannot attain control of the household resources because these are being delegated to the male relatives. If, in the absence of the husband, the wife is deprived of participation in family and community decision-making processes as well as in direct benefit from the remittances, she is adversely affected by the migration. Women may also find it difficult to cope with numerous family responsibilities without the support of their husbands such as in raising and educating the children. Apart from economic reasons, which are of primary importance, women and in particular young single women, tend to migrate in order to escape the hardship of rural life and the patriarchal and social control. In the course of their migration women may develop their skills and decide to build an independent life rather than resume their former roles in the household. However, since women in their migration rely on social networks that assist them in finding a job and in providing a safety net in times of emergencies, their ability to act independently may be curtailed or weakened.

Therefore, they may not fully benefit from the opportunities the migratory process brings, such as exposure to new values, ideas, roles and market demands. With increased demand for cheap female labor and aggressive job advertising on the part of prospective employers, rural women who are relatively isolated from the outside world are faced with the risks of trafficking and HIV/AIDS. The international community, including the United Nations system addressed this issue on various occasions. Men and women migrants often have to renegotiate their position within the relationship, household and community upon their return. Men tend to resume their decision-making position in the household more easily than women, if they wish so. On the other hand, long-term migrants often do not wish to resume their traditional work and prefer to engage in different activities that earn better income or bring higher status. The implication for households is that women continue to fulfill these tasks. For example, in western Sudan returning male migrants prefer to engage in trade rather than resume agricultural work in order to maintain their income. Rural migrants generally return home with new skills, work experiences, ideas, savings and technologies. At times the values women bring back home are more conservative. Such has been the case of Egyptian women returning from the Gulf countries. More often than not, however, women come home with greater self-confidence and higher self-esteem. In the Philippines, returning women overseas contract workers are beginning to engage in community affairs and politics. As with women migrants elsewhere, indigenous women migrants in Mexico come home more inclined to challenge the established gender roles and prevailing customs in the family. They are less likely to fit into their former roles and tend to abandon more easily local traditions because of their more restrictive nature for women than men. This may create strong conflicts leading to women's re-migration. The pressure to leave again tends to be strong when the money sent home by a female migrant has been used differently than she anticipated (spent rather than saved or invested). This leaves her with neither savings nor an economic base for the future, which for single women can diminish their prospects of getting married and for women with economic dependants, could mean going back to the starting point. Generally, remittances from migrants improve the quality of life of rural households, although their long-term impact and importance for sustaining rural life differ. A distinction can be made between remittances which are being used to feed the household members and remittances used for investments purposes.

The impact of remittances on household well being depends very much on who in the household control income. There is a tendency that income controlled by women is usually invested in the household and its members, and less on consumer items. Male remittances tend to arrive less regularly than those of women, and men take a larger share of their earnings income for their own personal use (alcohol, second wife, cigarettes) than women who are more likely to invest in production inputs (cattle, paying of debts, fertilizers and the such). Men tend to buy consumer items such as radio, bicycles, and cars, even in instances when their income may be needed for household survival. The remittances sent by daughters tend to be more regular, in particular if it is a transfer from woman to woman. Research has also shown that in some cases young and unmarried women have tended to keep a larger portion of their income for themselves.

D. Household dynamics

Globalization is associated in many places with an emerging diversity of household types, changes in decision-making, gender division of labor and intra-household relations. *Changes in the structure of rural households.* The emerging diversity of household types includes an increasing number of households headed by women as well as those containing multi-generations. There are also households which remain closely linked even though the members are split as a result of migration (multi-spatial households). The precise structure of multi- generational households varies. Apart from the typical extended family set-up, multi- generational households may include additional kin or may have a missing middle generation due to out-migration or HIV/AIDS related death, particularly in Africa. This results in a growing number of households in which grandmothers, single mothers or even children are looking after extended households which also include non-family members. Female-headed households (FHH) need to be recognized as a separate category including single person-households, and two and three generational households. Where men are away on temporary and seasonal migration, headship may be of temporary nature. It is also in these households that the men may continue to maintain the decision-making power. But there is a tendency of the development of female-headed households without a link to a male partner either because the woman is not married, is widowed, divorced or abandoned. It is in these households that female headship induces long-term changes in household structures. In these households women have the decision-making power and the full social and economic responsibility for the well being of its members. When women migrate, they tend to maintain close links with their rural homes with reciprocal benefits, for example, sending cash remittances and bringing back food to urban areas. Despite migration, the links between the members of the household remain. These intra household links also facilitate transfer of new ideas and cultural norms, values and habits. When men migrate, they often establish secondary households with new partners. This reduces remittances back to the rural areas and may create household conflicts.

As already discussed, one effect of globalization is a sharp increase in the diversification of different types of work household members may engage in. This as well as changes in household structure are affecting the division of labor within households. The opening up of new opportunities, such as wage labor, high value crop production or income generating activities can increase economic returns but would also increase the demand for labor. The majority of rural households respond by restructuring their household division of labor where women and children may be disproportionately burdened. Child labor for poor rural households is particularly important for achieving livelihood security. Children, in many instances escaping the social and legal factors that restrict the work options for adult women and men, are able to go just about anywhere and do any type of work, such as working as porter, shoe shiner, street vendor. Women's labor is particularly indispensable and often irreplaceable in rural areas. While men might be able to shift their work performance in accordance with the available work opportunities, women do not have the same flexibility. Productive labor of rural women includes non-remunerated family labor (unpaid family work) and paid labor (wage labor and piece rate work). In household production rural women's work is characterized as "multi-tasking" and "labor intensive" as they shoulder the responsibility for productive and reproductive tasks. Yet, policy makers do not adequately recognize the contribution of women and children to rural economies. Although there has been some progress in including women's unpaid work in official statistics, in most countries this issue is not recognized. In resource rich areas, certain industrial and manufacturing firms locate their production facility absorbing local labour. Location of such enterprises also capture state subsidies and various services. These new enterprises, while offering rural employment, also siphon resources such as fertile land, water for irrigation, and forest, that were crucial for traditional rural household production and for ensuring food security for many families. In such situations the burden of compensating for these resources often fall on the households, namely women who should spend more time and energy looking for these resources. The process of migration also has mixed impact on the situation of women in rural households. Migration of some family members may increase household income, but it can also cause an increase in women's workload. The impact of the additional workload on women is particularly strongly felt in areas where social support systems and services are weak or have eroded. Often children, particularly girls, are then called upon to assume some of the domestic tasks. Women employ different strategies to compensate the loss of labor. They may organize labour exchange with other women, work longer hours themselves or, if they have means from remittance and other income sources, hire additional labor. But they might also adopt such strategies as reducing the area under cultivation, switching to less labor-intensive but also less nutritious crops. The influence of women on the decision-making process in the household and in the community is a reflection of customs and cultures and of power relations. These relations are deeply embedded in society and are resistant to change. However, globalization is having a major impact on customary decision-making patterns. Changes in household structures have implied renegotiations of gender relations, with outcomes dependent on individual choices, socio-cultural context as well as economic factors. This may result in the possibility for increase in psychological problems and increased violence against women. In the context of improvement in women's economic position, women are more likely to control resources that directly affect all household members. This may enable women to take on a more active role in male dominated decision-making structures. It may also influence their social relations at the household and community level. Woman's role may no longer be only defined by her relationship to a man as his wife and mother of children but as a person influencing community matters or as a person engaging in a wide range of enterprises and social activities. This is reflected by rural women's participation in revolving credit schemes, cooperative ventures and increased networking at the work place as well as the participation in adult education and community programmes. Information technology has also impacted directly and indirectly on rural women. Many have access to radio and at times television. This has brought about a dramatic increase of information into their homes and has introduced them to patterns of gender relations and decision- making which exist in other cultures.

In many countries, the most visible change, which is taking place with regard to gender relations relate to marriage. As rural women adjust to economic change and as a result of earning an independent income and gaining access to new ideas or lifestyles, the factors influencing her choice of a partner or form of cohabitation tend to alter. For example, she may place more emphasis on personal characteristics rather than on economic prospects and cultural expectations. Worldwide there are a growing number of women choosing to delay marriage or remain single while still choosing to have children. There are communities in which migrant unmarried women returning home are looked at as particularly desirable marriage partner due to their economic independence, skills and abilities. There are, however, also communities in which these gains are perceived as a threat making it more difficult for the women to get married and readjust to the community. Women sex workers are particularly vulnerable to acts of harassment. Migrant women returning home are forced to adopt to the prevalent norms of gender relations and in the course of readjustment may be subject to total subservience to male family members. The greater the degree of exposure rural women have to cultural and social changes in the rest of the world, including human rights instruments, the more likely it is that these changes will also shape and reinforce their independent decision- making roles and influence gender relations. The impact of globalization has also brought about changes in the nature of local government, with rural women being drawn into decision-making structures on account of their new influence in the household and the community. This is also reflected in the conscious efforts of political parties to recruit rural women as candidates in all levels of politics. However, they are often not promoted within party structures to decision -making positions without some form of intervention.

Key findings

The analysis presented in this chapter has identified the following major impacts of globalization on the situation of rural women.

- Globalization has been associated with increased feminization of the labor force, as the female share of employment has increased worldwide. Much of the increase has resulted from a movement of female labor from the subsistence sector in rural areas to the paid economy.

- While new economic opportunities for rural women may have resulted from globalization, the benefits accruing to women and men differ due to constraints posed by their differential access to resources and by the gender norms that shape their willingness and capacity to take advantage of non-traditional job opportunities or new production technologies.

- Even within the context of production diversification most households in rural areas still depend on land, and natural resources for their livelihood, though not exclusively. In this context, it is disconcerting to note that the currently accelerated process of land titling, privatization of common property and land consolidation for efficient production, can increase the risk of women losing the existing property rights.

- Globalization has opened up opportunities for rural women into various types of paid non-farm activities. Since many of these activities are dependent on the natural resource base, it is a matter of some concern that intensive production and harvesting of forests for global markets have led to the degradation of critical natural resources.

- A renewed interest in bio-diversity and indigenous plants and materials have created opportunities for rural women to utilize their traditional knowledge and experience to take advantage of emerging national and global markets. However, these possibilities may not be realized unless Trade–Related Intellectual Property Rights are implemented in a transparent and just manner to protect the rights of local communities to indigenous resources.

- The move towards export-oriented industries based on unskilled labor has opened up many new employment opportunities for rural women. However, as the globalizing economies move on to more advanced forms of specialization requiring skilled labor, there is a danger that women will lose out at that stage unless appropriate actions are taken, well in advance, to enable them to acquire education and the requisite skills.

- One of the consequences of increasing migratory flows is that the absence of a husband or male member of the household often results in women taking over his tasks and responsibilities. While this means increasing women's burden, it may have empowering effects as this affords a woman the opportunity to acquire new skills and capacities.

- When remittance income permits, some women are able to hire labor reducing their work burden. However, in the absence of the husband, when the woman has to move in with her husband's relatives or patriarchal control is passed on to other male relatives, the women cannot attain control of the household resources, thus, being adversely affected by her husband's migration.

- When women migrate in search of new job opportunities, they may develop the skills and decide to build an independent life rather than resume their former roles in the household upon their return. Women tend to migrate using a network that assists them in finding a job and serves as a safety net in times of emergencies. However, such a network can also weaken their ability to utilize the opportunities the migratory process brings along such as becoming exposed and accustomed to new values, roles and market demands.

- In general both men and women have to renegotiate their positions within the relationship, household and community, upon their return. When women migrants return, they generally are less likely to fit into their former roles and tend to abandon more easily local traditions, supposedly because of their more restrictive nature for women than men. They are also more inclined to challenge the established gender roles and prevailing customs in the family. This may create strong conflicts leading to women's re -migration. Long-term male migrants, however, often do not wish to resume their traditional work and prefer to engage in other activities.

- One effect of globalization is a sharp increase in the diversification of the different types of work household members engage in. This as well as changes in household structure are affecting the division of labor within households sometimes leading to increasing work burden for women. This tendency has been reinforced by increasing migration of male family members. The impact of the additional workload on women is particularly strongly felt in areas where social support systems and services are weak or eroded. Often children, particularly girls, are then called upon to assume some of the domestic tasks.

- Globalization has given way to conditions that have the potential to significantly alter customary decision-making structures within the household. Changes in household structures have implied re -negotiation of gender relations, with outcomes dependent on individual choices, socio-cultural context as well as economic factors.
- Some rural women have become the only breadwinners in the household, as male members have become unemployed due to the displacement effect of labor markets. While this situation has enabled women to gain greater access to decision making power, at the same time, it has increased the possibility for greater exposure to violence.

- By and large, however, women's involvement in non-traditional activities and paid employment has changed the patterns of decision-making within rural households. From being passive participants in male-dominated decision-making structures, women are now gaining control of resources that directly affect them and other members of the household.

- One of the consequences of globalization has been greater exposure of rural women to cultural and social changes taking place in the rest of the world, including international human rights instruments. It is likely that these changes may shape and reinforce their independent decision-making roles. In some countries, current changes in the nature of local governance have increased the potential for women to be drawn into decision-making structures.

RECOMMENDATIONS

The implementation of these recommendations, at all levels, should be based on women's needs and priorities as identified by participatory rural processes and should focus on the following areas:

A. Human rights and labor standards

Women's views should be taken into account by Governments and Parliaments in the formulation of new laws and regulations, and in changing existing laws which contravene the principle of equality between women and men. Practical measures for the implementation of international instruments should be promoted. All relevant human rights instruments should be fully applied to rural women by Governments. Particular attention should be given to the implementation of art. 14 of CEDAW by States Parties to the Convention The Committee on the Elimination of Discrimination against Women (CEDAW) should develop a general recommendation on art.14 of the Convention and specifically request the reporting Governments to pay attention to the situation of rural women in the context of globalization. Women's equal right to property and inheritance should be fully and unconditionally recognized and implemented. Compliance with international standards of equality, including women's property rights, should be protected and promoted by Governments. Governments, international organizations including the UN system and NGOs should promote awareness of rural women's legal property rights as a priority, through: a) dissemination of national and international legal instruments; b) legal literacy training for rural women; c) legal assistance d) awareness raising of current discrimination e) gender sensitive training for implementers. ILO conventions as well as international standards of gender equality and human rights should be incorporated in national laws and codes of conduct of transnational corporations. Their observance should be monitored by Governments, relevant international organizations (e.g. ILO), trade unions, NGOs and other actors in civil society. Training programmes and discussions aimed at both rural women and men to promote gender awareness should be organized by national and local Governments, human rights groups and other NGOs to encourage the sharing of parental roles and household duties by men. Governments should eliminate de jure and/or de facto job discrimination against rural migrants and abolish all discriminatory regulations affecting living and working opportunities of rural migrants in urban areas, where appropriate. Governments, human rights and women's groups should provide information to rural migrant women on their human rights and international standards of equality. Governments should also provide these women with legal and consular support, as appropriate.

B. Women's livelihood and work

Governments, the private sector and civil society should jointly develop policies and projects and consolidate resources in order to improve infrastructures and provide job opportunities in rural areas. The functioning of financial institutions in rural areas should be analyzed by Governments and local authorities with the view to make them more accessible to rural women. This should include the support to revolving credit systems which are well suited to assist cooperative ventures in rural areas. Governments, donors, NGOs and the private sector should develop specific assistance programmes and advisory services to enhance rural women's economic skills in banking, modern trading and financial procedures matching requirements of the market economy. International donors should provide aid programmes directly to rural women rather than through the intermediaries. Governments should protect, through proper policy regulations, national resources and bio-diversity and invest in eco- and cultural tourism in rural areas to enable rural women to develop new economic activity. Rural women's indigenous knowledge and experience in subsistence production and environment should be recognized by national and local Governments as a resource and integrated into formal programmes. Support for rural women by Governments, NGOs and the private sector should not be confined to micro-enterprises. Rather, it should be directed at different scales of enterprise and women should be supported to expand their enterprises according to their needs and the possibilities in the given environment. In order to enhance women's participation in the labor market, improve their bargaining power and facilitate social contacts, Governments, NGOs and the private sector should support initiatives aimed at strengthening social networks that are a source of support and information.

C. Empowerment and capacity building through access to training, technology and basic services

Governments, NGOs, mass media and other actors in civil society should organize educational and awareness raising campaigns aimed at the transformation of cultural norms towards gender equality and encourage the private and public sector to be more gender-sensitive. Education, information and training for rural women should continue to be a high priority. Information services for rural women entrepreneurs should be expanded based on an analysis of rapidly changing and new market opportunities. Agricultural training programmes and educational institutions should revise their curriculum and methods of their work to respond to the needs of rural women in a rapidly changing global context. They should also provide rural women with information on emerging job opportunities. Governments and local authorities should develop exchange programmes at school level for rural and urban girls, to familiarize them with the living conditions in each sphere, and introduce them to the opportunities in each area. Governments, international organizations, including UN system, educational institutions and NGOs should create opportunities for rural women from various regions and countries to exchange experiences and information, to network, and engage in mutually beneficial projects. Rural women should be more actively supported by Governments and the private sector in gaining access to opportunities provided by new agriculture and information and communication technologies (ICT). These ICT facilities must penetrate to the level of rural villages. Governments should ensure provision of basic services in education and health, including maternal and child care services and devise them in accordance with the needs of rural women and girls including through distance and informal education programmes. The private sector should support such activities. Governments and the private sector should provide support for community initiatives for care of abandoned and/or orphaned children and other vulnerable members of the community. In order to improve rural women's negotiating positions and skills within the household and community, to strengthen their self-esteem, self-confidence and awareness of their rights, national and local Governments, international organizations and NGOs should provide capacity building training to the rural women. Governments, political parties, local authorities and NGOs should: (a) Facilitate women's participation in decision-making bodies at the local level by providing training and capacity building programmes. Quota system should be adopted as an interim measure, as appropriate. (b) Support and encourage rural women's equal participation in leadership in rural producer associations.

D. Migration and gender relations

NGOs should organize training programmes for women who are entering 'male working domains' and strengthen women's ability to cope with the absence of male members of the household and encourage them to perform all tasks related to new work requirements. Governments in cooperation with the International Migration Organization (IMO) should promote establishment of training programmes, services and community centers for migrant rural women. Governments, financial institutions and NGOs should provide rural communities and migrant women with information on modern ways of financial management, banking and investment opportunities in order to make their remittances and savings rewarding Donors should provide financial support to non-governmental organizations involved in providing direct counseling to female migrants from rural areas. In view of increased trafficking in women and children, Governments, international organizations and national and international law enforcement agencies should provide effective protection of rural women migrants and their children and protect their rights.

E. Further research and policy formulation

Governments, international organizations, including the UN system and research institutes should undertake analysis of the impact of 'globalization' on the rural population from a gender perspective. The data and information should be disaggregated by region and sex and made context-specific in order to reflect rural women's work including in the informal sector. It should be followed by further empirical research and case studies in various economic and socio cultural contexts, in order to assess the challenges to and opportunities for rural women. Governments and international organizations including the UN system should intensify their efforts to reflect women's unpaid work in rural households in national statistics and in policy formulation, implementation, and monitoring. The consequences of the photo sanitary regulations and subsidies to agriculture, as applied by some countries, should be analyzed by Governments, international organizations and research institutes to illustrate their impact on agriculture in developing countries and rural women in particular. The changing nature of households and gender relations in rural areas within the current global context should be studied by research institutes in order to enable Governments and international organizations to adjust policies and programmes to respond to rural women's needs. Further comparative long-term research should be conducted by IMO, national and international research institutes to document the diversified patterns of migration and their impact on gender relations and gender identities throughout the migration cycle. Special studies should be undertaken by Governments, research

institutes and the private sector to establish the best model for integrating rural women in the ICT field.
(*International Journal of Peace Studies, Volume 9, Number 1, Spring/Summer 2004*)

Chapter 6
GLOBALIZATION AND CONFLICT RESOLUTION

In this chapter the author consider the interplay between conflict and globalization, arguing that the interaction between globalization and conflict is complex. While much has been written on how globalization generates or accentuates conflict little has been written on how conflict and globalization interact to produce both positive and negative results. Theorists and practitioners in many fields are coming to terms with globalization, though perhaps with varying success. Later than some, scholars of peace and conflict resolution have begun to ask what globalization means to them. Though promising, this is a challenging task since the subject is, at best, multi-dimensional, and at worse, several distinct processes. Or, put another way, in the world today there are a number of globalization "discourses", and there may, in fact, be several different "globalizations". Many view globalization as a source of, or contributing factor to, conflict (Attali, 1991; Barber, 1995; Lerche, 1998; Scholte, 1997; Waters, 1995); and there are numerous case studies of the destabilizing impact of economic and cultural forces, radiating from the West, on local politics and culture in such places as Iran, Sierra Leone, or Indonesia (among others). Yet, this is a one-sided view of globalization and conflict, and the true relationship is more complex and subtle. For instance, one author, (Lerche, 1998: 47) while conceding that "...globalization is often disruptive and inequitable in its effects..."and that it has "...posed new challenges for existing public institutions..."; suggests that it has also, paradoxically, opened avenues for the excluded and marginalized to organize and protest against "...its subordinating and homogenizing force." In a somewhat similar vein we argue that the relationship between globalization and conflict is complex in ways not heretofore fully discussed in the literature. Globalization, understood broadly, is an accelerator of social change, and as such, may act as a catalyst for conflict, aggravating the tensions in any given society and even creating new ones. At the same time, it may also catalyze and accelerate conflict. Thus the intensifying interconnectedness which characterizes globalization has unintended consequences for both conflict and peace processes; and here we explore this theme in some depth. After defining what we mean by globalization, we go on to examine its relationship with conflict and its interaction with conflict prevention and resolution.

Aspects of Globalization

Globalization has come to mean many things to many people. In this regard, one author (Riggs, 2003) argues that "dimensions" of globalization central to the concerns of no less than seven academic disciplines can be distinguished.1 Our concern here is primarily with the direct and indirect effects of what has come to be known as "economic", "market-driven" or "neo-liberal" globalization. However, it is impossible to limit our discussion to economic processes, narrowly defined, since the same forces and enabling conditions that have led to global economic change have also facilitated change in other areas. Specifically, economic perspectives on globalization view it to be rooted in changes in technology and production processes. The emergence of a global division of labor and a more open and less regulated world economy are viewed as its products. The 'globalization as economics' thesis actually has two versions, the relatively benign and the malevolent. The relatively benign thesis of globalization as economics posits that with the growing complexity of and interdependence of the world economy there are emerging centers of consumption and production that are no longer bounded by nation states (Reich, 1991; Ohmae, 1990, 1995; Friedman, 1999). For example, middle range information technology production centers have emerged in Dublin, San Francisco, Delhi, Singapore and Sydney, and financial, human, and intellectual capital flow freely from one location to the next. Nation-states have little or no control over this movement of capital, thereby losing the ability to regulate their economies. This view to a large degree assumes globalization to be a natural and inevitable process having unintended, but generally positive, consequences. The malevolent version of globalization as economics sees technological change and capital mobility as producing a number of undesirable effects (Castells, 1993). For instance, companies can take advantage of local conditions and move production facilities in response to changing local conditions – regardless of the impact of these changes on local populations. A factory in Indonesia may be profitable today, but less so tomorrow. Perhaps it will be moved to India or Mexico, depending upon the corporate financial ledger. Seen from this perspective, globalization is the latest stage in the development of capitalism; a stage in which freely moving capital working through multinational corporations has succeeded in imposing its priorities on nation-states and local populations. In either case, the focus of globalization here is on economics, and it is portrayed as unidirectional. Another strand of this literature critiques the positing of globalization as a natural and inevitable process. Some like Robert Cox (1996), critique what they call an "ideology" of globalization that presents it as inevitable and beneficial. For them this ideology underplays the unevenness of the process (which is both economically and politically driven) and the inequality between states and actors who are caught up in it (Hurrell and Woods, 1995). In reality, some peoples, localities, or institutions are more affected by globalizing forces than others. Some areas will benefit economically, others will not; certain groups will feel invaded by alien cultural forms, whereas others will be untouched. The great divide between those benefiting from globalization and those hurting from it accentuates the possibilities for conflict. More generally, Held et al. (2000) argue that globalization creates new spatial organizations and social relations defined in terms of four key factors:

- *Extensity* is the stretching of social, political, and economic activities across frontiers and borders. An event in one region has impacts elsewhere, so for example changes in share prices in New York may lead to women in Malaysia losing their job in a shoe manufacturing plant.
- *Intensity* is more than occasional interconnectedness, as it refers to a growing number of interconnections. The number of relationships between events, institutions and people in San Francisco and Santiago, Chile are increasing.
- *Velocity* is the speed of interactions. Thus, not only is the rate at which the interconnectedness between Santiago and San Francisco increasing, but the time taken to establish connections is constantly shrinking.
- *Impact* is the deepening of extensity, intensity and velocity. Distant events have greater local consequences. As globalization accelerates change along all four vectors, new regional and global networks of activity, interaction and the use of power come into being – in each instance creating new sets of "winner" and "losers". The authors of this model acknowledge that globalization concerns more than economics. They recognize that its direction is not exclusively from the economically well off Western world to the poorer non-western world. Rather, anyone who can access the technology of globalization can influence the process(es). The actors in this globalized world are diverse, and include multi-national companies, communal and religious groups, diasporas, publics, nation states, and more. In contrast to the state-centric perspective characteristic of international relations, in the study of globalization we find that the relative importance of one actor versus another varies from situation to situation, from context to context. This leads to an important insight: the conceptually interesting area in the study of globalization and conflict is the global – local interaction. Global forces may bring a new set of actors to bear on a local situation, by facilitating the expression of a local conflict, contributing to its resolution, or even changing its character and outcome in other unpredictable ways. The literature on conflict and globalization has shed some light on these dynamics. However, what has not

received as much attention is analysis of possible links between globalization and conflict resolution and prevention. Therefore, the discussion that follows is an initial attempt to assess to what extent and in what ways globalization, conflict, and conflict resolution interact.

Conflict and Globalization

Globalization may influence the expression of conflict in a number of ways, including disturbing b local events, providing new resources over which to compete, and threatening deeply held values or symbols, to name a few. We have selected two cases to illustrate these connections. One particularly troublesome example of how globalization and conflict interact can be found in the story of 'conflict diamonds', where diamonds are used to fund military operations. Diamonds have long been valuable commodities. In 1999 trade in raw, unpolished diamonds totaled some $7.25 billion (Goreux, 2001:3). It is truly a globalized market. Dominated by the South African DeBeers cartel (owning some 40% of the world's diamond mines), diamonds may be mined in southern Africa, Russia, Canada, or Australia. Raw diamonds are polished in Antwerp, London, Bombay or Dubai. Polished diamonds are then exported for sale largely in Japan or the U.S. (Goreux, 2001). It is estimated that the trade in 'conflict diamonds' amounts to some $250 million. While only 3.5% of the total trade in diamonds, it represents a significant source of income for warring parties. In Angola and Sierra Leone, the failure of the central government, insurgency campaigns, and the lack of external funding sources have combined with the access to diamond mining regions to create a disaster. In Angola, UNITA (the rebel force led by the late Jonas Savimbi, seeking to oust the current government in Luanda) lost financial support from the U.S. government, after the end of the Cold War. To replace this funding UNITA first stockpiled diamonds and then used diamond sales to fund weapons purchases, in order to continue its war. In Sierra Leone the Revolutionary United Front (RUF) has been waging war against the central government since

1991. The RUF relies upon diamond smuggling to support its military campaign. This military campaign has resulted in the death of some 10,000 to 20,000 people and seen nearly 2 million people displaced. In a further twist, al-Qaeda is believed to use the 'conflict diamond' smuggling route to launder its own proceeds. It is alleged that al-Qaeda operatives purchase diamonds in Africa, export them and convert them into cash as needed (Farah, 2001:A1). Alan Tidwell and Charles Lerche.

A diamond on the finger of a casualty of the attack on the World Trade Center may well have once been traded by al-Qaeda and mined by those working with the RUF. While 'conflict diamonds' account for a very small portion of the total global trade in uncut diamonds, the diamonds play a central role in funding two bloody and violent conflicts. In addition, 'conflict diamonds' create an incentive among some to keep a place like Sierra Leone mired in violence. The global market in diamonds, interacting with the global arms trade, has impacted local conditions in Angola and Sierra Leone. In both nations the local conflicts have been fed, and new dynamics introduced. A second example of the interplay between globalization and conflict is found in Ambon in Maluku province, Indonesia, which has been the site of sectarian violence since 1999. Unlike Sierra Leone and Angola, there is no strong separatist movement there.2 Elsewhere in Indonesia there are some active separatist movements in Aceh and Irian Jaya, for example. Instead, the conflict in Maluku represents communal tensions between Muslims and Christians. Maluku, formerly the Moluccas, or Spice Islands, has been home to a large Christian population as well as Muslims. In recent years the Muslim population has grown due to internal migration. In years past, Christians received favorable treatment from colonial masters, leaving them in charge of the local bureaucracy and economy. Conflict erupted in 1999, tapping into undercurrents and led to riots, leaving hundreds dead. Since then some 5000 have died in the ensuing violence (International Crisis Group [ICG], 2002:1). In 2002 parties to the conflict signed the Indonesian government brokered Malino II Peace Agreement, which appears (at this writing) to be shaky as there has been renewed violence in Maluku. The interplay between the forces of globalization and conflict are apparent to the observer, though they are less spectacular than in the 'conflict diamonds' case. In the Maluku example democratization and marketization, two prominent reform "themes" promoted worldwide by several of the leading economic and military powers in the world, interacted with local conflict dynamics. Chua (1998) argues that democratization and marketization create the basis for provoking and heightening ethnic conflict, and her logic is equally applicable to religious as well as ethnic groups in post-colonial Indonesia. Chua's thesis is that marketization benefits some more than others, a theme echoed by many other critics of liberal market reforms. Furthermore, in the developing world ethnically divided societies are often characterized by one ethnic group gaining politically through majority rule, while a different group gains economically. The result of this is that the group in political power is not the group with economic power, and this tends to rigidify ethnic boundaries and establish competitive relationships. According to Chua's thesis, marketization, democratization, and ethnic division combine to create potentially explosive social conditions. Indonesia, an ethnically divided society, has been trying to democratize since the fall of the Suharto's New Order regime in 1998. One aspect of this program has been a process of political decentralization. The then Indonesian Minister for Home Affairs and Regional Autonomy Surjadi Soedirdje explained that decentralization was a significant component of democratic reform in Indonesia (Soedirdje, 2000). In addition, the World Bank and various donor nations favored decentralization. Through devolving many powers to the local level and giving greater value to local elections the process of decentralization increased rivalries as local politicians vied for power. While local in effect, it is important to remember that decentralization was implemented at least in part as a response to outside influences. Marketization, including extensive privatization of ownership, is also under way in Indonesia at the urging of both the World Bank and the International Monetary Fund (IMF). Thus, Indonesia, according to Chua's (1998) argument, had all the ingredients for heightened ethnic conflict, and this seems to be born out in the cases of Aceh, Irian Jaya, and Maluku. Divisions have existed in Maluku for some years and are illustrated by what happened in Ambon, in Maluku. The conflict finds its roots in the divide between the largely Christian indigenous Ambonese and the largely migrant Muslim populations. While in the town of Ambon Christians are in slight majority (just over 50%), Muslims (roughly 60%) dominate the rest of Maluku (ICG, 2002). Generally, the newer Moslem populations have done better economically than historically prosperous Christian populations. In fact, there had been a general diminution of Christian prosperity and political power. The gradual shift in political power was reinforced by developments at the national level in the 1990's as then President Soeharto attempted to mobilize\ Muslim support. In Maluku he appointed Muslim Ambonese governors for the first time, and Muslims obtained more positions in the local bureaucracy. After Soeharto's fall and with the approach of national and provincial elections in June 1999, political tensions rose as displaced Christians attempted to win back influence, particularly through the Partai Dmokrasi Indonesia – Perjuangan (PDIP) led nationally by Megawati Soekarnoputri (ICG, 2002:2). By 2000 the conflict had exploded into a full-blown melee, with both sides engaged in acts of extreme violence and cruelty. One of the local messages that emerged from the conflict between Muslims and Christians was that Christians were persecuting the Muslims. As a consequence Laskar Jihad, a Java-based militia arrived in Ambon to reinforce local Muslim groups. Global discourse and ideologies of democratization, decentralization, and marketization have in combination made impressions upon Ambon/Maluku. While tensions may have already existed between Muslims and Christians in Ambon/Maluku, they had not yet been expressed through overt violence. However, marketization and democratization appear to have redistributed wealth and political influence in ways that widened the gulf and increased the polarization between these two communities. Both the 'conflict diamonds' and Maluku cases illustrate ways in which globalization and conflict interacts negatively. In these examples global market forces and international pressures for democratic and liberal economic reforms exacerbated already brewing local conflicts. We now look at globalization's impact on conflict *resolution*, and the results are more mixed.

Conflict Resolution and Globalization

The interaction between the global and the local can create unintended processes of resolution. Through creating new means or motivation for dialogue among contending parties, globalization can be a "spark" for peace. In the conflict on Bougainville, Papua New Guinea (PNG), for instance, globalization contributed both to conflict and to its resolution. Conflict in Bougainville erupted in the late 1980's as separatist groups in Bougainville opposed mining at Panguna, an operation owned by Conzinc RioTinto Australia or CRA (now Rio Tinto). The Bougainville Revolutionary Army (BRA) engaged in acts of violence aimed at closing down the mine, an end they achieved. The mine was of some importance to the Papua New Guinea government in Port Moresby, in as much as it accounted for about 17% of government revenues. The mine came into being following the Bougainville Copper Agreement of 1974; this agreement created grounds for conflict in Bougainville by replacing local custom with regard to land tenure and ownership with the Australian national practice of "what's under the ground belongs to the government". This change effectively excluded traditional land owners from the process of regulating who used the mineral wealth of Bougainville. Other causes of the Bougainville conflict outlined by Regan (1999) include:

- Resentment of landowners over establishment of the mine and its impact on them and their physical environment;

- Inter-generational conflict among landowners near the mine over distribution of rents, compensation, and other benefits from the mine;
- Resentment among Bougainvillean employees of Bougainville Copper Ltd about perceived limited opportunities for promotion;
- Economic nationalism, or for the Bougainvillian economy to be dominated by Bougainvillians;
- Tensions caused by the collapse of cocoa prices between 1987 and 1988 (this was a society heavily dependent on small-holder cocoa production);
- Resentment of the increasing numbers of outsiders coming to Bougainville;
- Ethnicity, where there are numerous linguistic groups who vie for resources in Bougainville;
- Abuses of human rights perpetrated by members of the PNG security forces.

The outbreak of conflict led the PNG government to deploy the PNG Defence Force (PNGDF) in Bougainville. This led to bloody violence and the isolation of Bougainville by PNG. Yet, by 1996 the PNGDF was all but defeated by the BRA. In an effort to recoup their losses the PNG government of Sir Julius Chan sought to end the Bougainville conflict by using a mercenary firm, Sandline Corporation. Sandline was to go into Bougainville and impose a military solution. Upon discovery, however, MP's and the military revolted and brought down the Chan government. The event also catalyzed the BRA into taking action on seeking peace. By 1997 parties had established a sufficient level of trust to sign the Burnham Declaration, which outlines the early stages of a peace process. The New Zealand government worked with conflicting parties in Bougainville, bringing them to New Zealand for talks. The resulting Burnham Declaration was built upon with Burnham II and the Lincoln Agreement, all of which are designed to enhance trust and establish mechanisms to resolve local conflicts. The Bougainville case is an interesting one, in as much as it demonstrates how globalization can be both an influence for conflict escalation and de-escalation. Global copper trade was surely a key dynamic in bringing out the conflict, as the Panguna mine was responsible for some 17% of PNG's revenues. While multinational business interests certainly played a role in stimulating conflict, the Sandline affair and global economics also played a role in moving the conflict from escalation to de-escalation. The Sandline affair acted as a catalyst for parties to review their positions and seek alternatives to violence; and, the fact that those on Bougainville needed an income and that the mine was probably the most prominent export industry in the area acted as incentives to make peace. However, globalization may also interact with conflict resolution processes in negative ways, as illustrated by the case of East Timor. In a sense, the consequences of independence for East Timor were "globalized" or made relevant in capitals around the globe where secessionist movements existed, inhibiting negotiations with other separatist groups. Viewed from a globalization frame East Timor was an economic and political drain for Indonesia, especially after the financial collapse of 1997. It could be argued that with Indonesia in financial difficulty and feeling the pressure of U.S. Congressional concerns over human rights abuses, the Habibie government took the view that giving East Timor independence would be a wise step. The Habibie government's motivation could be seen as most calculating. Indonesia would always dominate tiny East Timor both politically and economically, whereas leaving a garrison force in East Timor to maintain formal political control would have been both expensive and inefficient. The rationale for giving up East Timor became even more compelling when the international community agreed to take on the costs of creating an independent state. The unanticipated consequence of East Timor's independence was, however, to fuel the fires of separatism in Indonesia and elsewhere. Separatists in Irian Jaya and Aceh pointed to the case of East Timor and sought to use it as an example of what could be accomplished through resistance and violence. This somewhat perverse result exemplifies the argument made by John Maynard Keynes in

1920 in his seminal work, *The Economic Consequences of Peace.* In his analysis of the economic and political consequences of the Versailles Treaty, he demonstrated that peace generally has both positive and negative consequences: these consequences may have a far reaching impact. Globalization may also bring about unexpected opportunities for resolution of local conflicts. In early August 1998 Australian Gas Light (AGL) announced its intention to construct a natural gas pipeline across rural Queensland in northeastern Australia. AGL's natural gas business was growing as world consumption of natural gas continued to expand. In an effort to meet both local and export demand AGL expanded its extraction activities. The proposed pipeline, however, crossed aboriginal traditional territory. In 1992 the High Court of Australia struck down the principle of *terra nullius*, in issuing their decision on *Mabo v. Queensland*; this established the legal right for indigenous people to claim traditional ownership of land.4 In 1993 the Australian Labor government introduced legislation, later to become the Native Title Act of 1993. The objects of the Act were the following:

to provide for the recognition and protection of native title; and

to establish ways in which future dealings affecting native title may proceed and to set standards for those dealings; and

to establish a mechanism for determining claims to native title; and

to provide for, or permit, the validation of past acts invalidated because of the existence of native title. In 1996 *Wik v. Queensland* found that native title may exist on pastoral leases. This decision led in turn to the Coalition government's Ten Point Plan and later authoring of the Native Title Amendment Act of 1998. This act altered the basis for native title claims, emphasizing that applications could be made on the part of a group and by those who could act as representatives of a group. Under both acts, applications to native title claims are to be negotiated. "'Negotiated agreements' (sometimes called 'negotiated settlements') come in a variety of different forms and are brought about by a number of different circumstances. As the National Native Title Tribunal described them, they 'may range from broad arrangements on a regional level to details of daily practices, such as closure of station gates and fire control'"(Doenau, 1999:7). Negotiation over native title is the essence of both the 1993 and 1998 Native Title Acts. The negotiations between AGL and representatives of the indigenous people occurred against the backdrop of calls for reconciliation between the Australian government and Aboriginal Australians. Specifically, calls were made by numerous indigenous groups for the government to issue an apology. A host of notable Australians, including the Governor General Sir William Deane, offered apologies. Thus, this negotiation resulted in both a contract for a natural gas pipeline and a forward step in the reconciliation process. One indigenous negotiator commented: The AGL pipeline ... has given Aboriginal people in this area a chance to honour those Heroes of the Dreamtime, and to return to their homelands. Though it was brief, it has awakened the Spirits of the Land and, for a time, we have rejoiced Now the way is paved for us to revisit our areas and gain strength in the knowledge that our Ancestors held on to our inner spirits, and the invisible string will continue to hold us to them and to our Lands (AGL internal document, undated). The global demand for natural gas, combined with the global trend to recognize indigenous land claims, interacted with local conflict, and the result contributed to a broader process of reconciliation in Australia. Indigenous negotiators, many of whom had never interacted with European descended Australians, had won recognition for their needs. In this case, globalization acted as a catalyst for both conflict resolution and peace building. Finally, globalization can generally bring about broader and more coordinated efforts in conflict prevention, through the expansion of information technology that links people together in action networks who were previously not able to be in regular contact with each other. Two different examples may suffice to illustrate how globalization may contribute to coordination on conflict prevention activities. In 2002 the Japan Center for Preventive Diplomacy hosted its second e-symposium on conflict prevention. The e symposium had roughly 500 registrants from around the globe. Participants came largely from the non-government organizations (NGOs) and academic sectors. Another initiative is the Transatlantic Internet Seminar Kosovo/a and Southeastern Europe (TISKSE). This Carnegie sponsored program is designed to link participants from academia and civil society in education about conflict prevention in the Balkans. It is too early to fully evaluate these initiatives, but they already illustrate the unprecedented impact and creative influence that focused applications of information technology – one "engine" of globalization – can have in the areas of conflict resolution, peace building, and early warning. Drawing on the examples from Bougainville, East Timor, Australia, and more generally those offered of global communication, globalization may speed or trigger resolution, may spread negative consequences of peace, and may facilitate conflict prevention coordination. It remains to assess what these findings mean for both the study and the practice of peace and conflict resolution.

Conclusion

With respect to peace and conflict resolution, our examples, while not comprehensive do provide initial evidence of the complex interaction between conflict and globalization. Globalization can act to catalyze conflict in a variety of settings. Global markets may provide under-funded and poor groups the financial means to purchase weapons. These global markets may actually help destabilize local conditions, as factions seek to exploit natural resources. The case of the 'conflict diamonds' is an excellent illustration of how markets can have a negative impact on local conflicts. Globalization may also introduce ideological themes into local politics. If acted upon and implemented through policy, these themes, such as marketization or democratization, may trigger ethnic and religious conflict, as in Maluku as groups vie for power and influence in a changing environment. Conflict resolution or de-escalation also appears to be impacted by globalization. The conflict in Bougainville demonstrated how globalization can help spark interest in bringing about a peaceful resolution to conflict. Peace agreements are not without their unintended consequences. Sometimes peace agreements, while positive and just in their own right, have unintended consequences. This was demonstrated by the case of East Timor. Interestingly, globalization can also foster peaceful resolution of local issues. The case of AGL and indigenous people negotiating over access to traditional land actually helped contribute to reconciliation efforts. Finally, the global diffusion of information technology can promote greater coordination among people by linking those interested in conflict prevention in ever-broader action networks. These findings indicate that the much talked about global "compression" of time and space occurs as much in conflict settings as in any other; and that, for reasons discussed above, they make predicting the course of conflict more complex. One cannot simply state that globalization will either escalate or de-escalate conflict. Rather, the manner in which the global and local interact must be considered on a case-by-case basis with the analyst teasing out the various interactions between them. For example, the relationship between marketization and democratization appears to be far more complex than first anticipated. While both are promoted as means to empower local populations, on the ground they may produce distinctly negative consequences. To reiterate, in this regard the problematic area is not democratization or marketization *per se*, but rather their interactions with local circumstances. Conflict resolution processes such as negotiation, mediation, or other third party processes may also be impacted by globalization. In the Australian example negotiators from both sides took a broad view, incorporating emerging global norms about the rights of indigenous people into the settlement. However, while this approach may work in some cases, it is not always a good idea, since outside influences may introduce issues that unnecessarily complicate agendas or have unforeseen negative consequences. Therefore, conflict resolution practitioners must be careful in managing global influences (to the degree possible), as well as local conditions, in any given context. Assuming our findings here are indicative, the issue remains of whether globalization is simply a "double-edged" sword, impacting conflict escalation and de-escalation more or less evenly; or whether it tends to foster more conflict than it resolves. This is an important question with far reaching implications for globalization discourse and global governance. Already we are entitled to be skeptical of claims that globalization is inherently positive and benign. If it can be demonstrated to be, on balance, negative, then laissez faire is an unacceptable policy stance, and the challenge of channeling at least certain key aspects of globalization in positive directions cannot long be avoided. Thus, more investigation needs to be undertaken into the complex relationship between globalization and conflict escalation and de-escalation.

References

1. 2002. "The Asian Front", *Washington Post,* January 27, p. B6.
2. Attali, Jacques. 1991. *Millenium: Winners and Losers in the Coming World Order.* New York: Times Books.
3. Barber, Benjamin R. 1995. *Jihad vs. McWorld.* New York: Times Books.
4. Castells, Manuel. 1993. "The International Economy and the New International Division of Labor". In Martin Carnoy, Stephen Cohen, and Fernando Herique Cardoso, eds., *The New Global Economy in the Information Age: Reflections on our Changing World.* University Park, Pa.: The Pennsylvania State University Press.
5. Cox, Robert W. 1996. "A Perspective on Globalization." In James H. Mittelman, ed., *Globalization: Critical Reflections.* Boulder: Lynne Rienner.
6. Chua, Amy L. 1998. "Markets, Democracy, and Ethnicity: Toward a New Paradigm for Law and Development," *The Yale Law Journal,* 108(1), October, pp. 1-108. Alan Tidwell and Charles Lerche.

7. Dicken, Peter. 1998. *Global Shift: Transforming the World Economy.* New York: Guilford Press.
8. Doenau, Stan. 1999. *Native Title and Negotiated Agreements.* Sydney: Edvance Publications.
9. Farah, Douglas. 2001. 'Al Qaeda Cash Tied to Diamond Trade Sale of Gems From Sierra Leone Rebels Raised Millions, Sources Say', *Washington Post,* November 2, p. A1.
10. Friedman, Thomas L. 1999. *The Lexus and the Olive Tree: Understanding Globalization.* New York: Farrar, Straus, Giroux.
11. Goreux, Louis. 2001. 'Conflict Diamonds', *World Bank Africa Region Working Paper Series,* Number 13, March, pp. 7–8 and 21-23.
12. Held, David, Anthony McGrew, David Goldblatt and Jonathan Perraton. 2000. "Rethinking Globalization." In David Held and Anthony McGrew, eds., *The Global Transformations Reader.* London: Blackwell Publishers.
13. Hurrell, Andrew and Ngaire Woods. 1995. "Globalisation and Inequality," *Millennium: Journal of International Studies,* 24 (3), pp. 447-471.
14. International Crisis Group. 2002. "Indonesia: The Search for Peace in Maluku", *ICG Asia Report Number 31,* Jakarta/Brussels, February 8, pp. 1-26.
15. Keynes, John Maynard. 1920. *The Economic Consequences of the Peace.* New York: Harcourt, Brace, and Howe.
16. Lerche III, Charles O. 1998. "The Conflicts of Globalization," *International Journal of Peace Studies,* 3 (1), January, pp. 47-66.
17. Ohmae, Kenichi. 1990. *The Borderless World: Power and Strategy in the Interlinked Economy.* New York: Free Press.
18. Reich, Robert B. 1991. *The Work of Nations.* New York: Alfred A. Knopf.
19. Regan, Anthony. 1999. *Bougainville: The Peace Process and Beyond,* Submission to the Foreign Affairs Sub-Committee of the Joint Standing Committee on Foreign

Affairs, Defence and Trade Inquiry, Canberra, Australia: June.

20. Scholte, Jan Art. 1997. "The Globalization of World Politics." In John Baylis and Steve Smith, eds., *The Globalization of World Politics.* Oxford: Oxford University Press.
21. Soedirdja, Surjadi. 2000. "Statement of the Government of Indonesia on Decentralization", Consultative Group Meeting on Indonesia, World Bank, Tokyo, October 17-18.
22. Waters, Malcolm. 1995. *Globalization.* London: Routledge.

Chapter 7
Tourism and Globalization in the Arab World

Living in a small village called the "world" where differences among nations are eroding is a reality that cannot be denied or ignored. The 'Globalization' as a phenomenon has been seen in most aspects of our life; the tremendous economic integration witnessed worldwide, the revolution of technology, the extensive usage of means of communication and transportation, the increasing opportunities for communities and nations across the borders to interact with each others, and many other aspects are now transforming our world into a small village where cultural differences are eroding. This chapter is discussing the relationship between globalization and tourism in regard to the impact caused by them, and more specifically in Arab countries (Middle East and North Africa regions). The main finding of this topic is that economic benefits of tourism supported by aspects of globalization, were basically the focus of Arab countries, less consideration was given to environmental and socio-cultural impacts caused by tourism due to the pace of development as well as low standard of living for locals in these countries; such finding initiates the need to conduct a more sustainable planning and development for tourism.

"Ideas of 'globalization' are so broad, so diverse and so changeable that it sometimes seems possible to pronounce virtually anything on the subject" (Scholte 1997: 427). Such statement reflects how it is difficult to find a definition that encounters all aspects related to globalization. Although of the widespread of this concept, even in the popular media, there are different definitions and conceptions that were put for this phenomenon (Cogburn 1998). Some of these definitions reflected a geographical aspect dealing with borders, Scholte

(2000: 16) for example refers to 'Globalization' as 'a process of removing restrictions on movements between countries in order to create an "open", "borderless" world economy'. In some other cases, there was a focus on the economic, cultural and social outspreads increasingly growing around the world. David Held et al (1999: 16) defined globalization as a ' process (or set of processes) which embodies a transformation in the spatial organization of social relations and transactions - assessed in terms of their extensity, intensity, velocity and impact - generating transcontinental or inter-regional flows and networks of activity'. The concept of 'Globalization' also can be referred to as the increasing integration of economies around the world, particularly through trade and financial flows, the concept is reflecting as well the movement of people (labor) and knowledge (technology) across international borders (IMF 2000). 'It is the ever-tightening network of connections which cut across national boundaries, integrating communities in new "space-time combinations' (Hall 1992: 299). Moreover, these communities are all forming a world that is a single interconnected and interdependent whole, a homogeneous mass or a single social order, caused by the erosion of local differences (Allen & Massey 1995). More simply and directly, it is all about spreading various objects and experiences to people all over the world (Scholte 2000). The previously mentioned definitions of globalization are all indicating the multidimensionality of such concept. Several interrelated aspects in our life are clearly seen in them; according to Scholte (1997), these aspects can be classified into six different groups; which are: The sphere of communications and media that allows a nearly immediate contact between individuals (e.g. such as air travel, telephony, computer networks, radio, and television); the spread and the expansion of business enterprises, civic associations and regulatory agencies, (i.e. organizations) that work within trans-border operations; the trade and movement of goods and services between countries, the spread of money via financial instruments (e.g. Eurobonds and many derivatives), and various monies (e.g. the US dollar and the Special Drawing

Right), which electronically circulate across the world in short spans of time; another main aspect is the inclusion of global cases in the process, such as stratospheric ozone depletion and the decline in biological diversity as results of accelerating development, which is not constrained by distance or circumscribed by borders. And finally, the widely shared vision by people around the world that it is a single place more than a globe divided into borders, this can be clearly seen through affiliating themselves into communities based on ideological and cultural aspects (e.g. of religious faith, race, etc.) Tourism (as a phenomenon) highly depends on the progress of communication and transportation, which are both reinforced by money movement and the distribution of companies (e.g. airlines and different transportation companies, hotel chains...etc); both exogenous and market factors have their significant role in shaping the development of tourism; for exogenous factors, demographic and social changes, economic and financial developments, transport infrastructure growth, technological development and development in trading, all have contributed to the growth in tourism as an industry. For market forces, the development seen in destination product, marketing, computer reservation systems, global destination databases, and operators' products, all led to the variation in tourism markets and options offered for them around the world (Gee 1997). It becomes logic then to consider tourism as a main component in the process of globalization. Moreover, the indicators of tourism industry growth characterized by receipts and flows of travelers stretching all over the globe, the increase of markets (tourists groups), the rapidity into which different destinations are drawn into tourism development, the increase in holiday destinations and distances between them; all are reflecting the progress witnessed in telecommunications, finance and transport, which are playing an instrumental role in the globalization of tourism (Mowforth & Munt 2003).

Globalization and Tourism

There are some driving forces of globalization that have their clear impact on tourism, travel and hospitality industries. The liberalization of air transport, liberalization of trade in services, and the spread of information and communication technologies, the extensive use of internet in sales and marketing of trips and tourism packages, all contribute to the continuous growth of tourism industry (ILO 2001). The global travel and tourism industries of the 21st century are mainly depending on civil aviation, this can be clearly seen through the calling of national governments and international and regional industry organizations for improved coordination between air transport, airport infrastructure, tourism investment and tourism development policies. Such improvements will increase the contribution of the travel and tourism industry to national economies and regional development, developed and developing countries vitally depending on tourism as a main source of wealth and job opportunities, and which are looking for foreign investment to better exploit and manage their natural, scenic, historical or cultural resources for tourism purposes, are now in the front line pushing for air transport liberalization (IVC 2006). Moreover, electronic technology is also facilitating this growth by giving access to fare and hotel information and online reservation services, another form of improvement countries are exploiting worldwide (UNESCO 1999). Tourism has grown in the past 10 years; about 880 million international arrivals were recorded in 2009, accounting for almost US$852 billion of receipts (UNWTO 2010). Moreover, it is predicted that more growth will take place, not only for those destinations receiving the highest numbers of tourists, but also for other ones with small market shares. According to WTO (2004) forecasts of the year 2020 predict that Europe, the Americas, and East Asia and the Pacific will account for 80% of total arrivals, other destinations as Africa and South Asia will also witness an increase in their arrivals as well (5.5% and 6% per year respectively), compared with a world average of just over

4%. In addition to being a vital source of income as seen from these indicators, it is also a major source of employment, according to a World Travel and Tourism Council (WTTC) estimates for the year 2009, about 77.3 million jobs were directly offered by tourism around the world, and 219.8 million (7.6 % of the world total) if all the indirect jobs opportunities of the sector are taken into account. Tourism also has a significant contribution of 9.4% of the world total GDP. For capital investment, private and public sectors combined are expected to spend US$ 1,220.1 billion worldwide (9.4%) of total investment. In 2009, the economic activity is expected to post US$7,340 billions as a total demand; this total demand is expected to grow to US$14,382 billion by 2019. Such growth indicators are giving uniqueness to tourism and travel industry as a development sector for many countries around the world. What also makes the growth of tourism also unique is its fast recovery after decline stages; for example, since the 1960's till this century, tourism has been growing in term of both arrivals and receipts, although of having some decreases that took place because of some crises within some particular years from 2001-03, travel and tourism worldwide suffered four depressing scourges – economic downturns or recessions in some major tourism generating markets, widespread terrorist attacks (9/11, Djerba, Bali, Mombasa, etc), subsequent military conflicts in Afghanistan and Iraq, and the SARS epidemic. But 2004 recorded the best annual growth in tourism of the last 20 years, with international tourist arrivals up 10 per cent over 2003's level (IVC 2006). Tourism has proved to be quick to recover, which increases its potential to be a vital source of economy. Another important factor that contributed to tourism growth is having substantial changes in tourist patterns and behavior were witnessed on international scale; these include the increased frequency of travel, but for shorter trips, in less expensive destinations closer to home, often involving lower categories of travel and accommodation; the high adoption of the new intra-regional routes offered by low-cost airlines (which have consolidated their position in Europe and are growing rapidly in Asia Pacific and the Middle

East); the wide spread of new travel patterns as 'do it yourself' and last-minute booking, stimulated and facilitated by the internet; and the aggressive price competition which has led to an increasing need for all industry players to innovate and diversify in terms of product development and marketing (IVC 2006). All of these indicators and changes are giving a strong evidence for the growing importance of tourism in the economy and development of countries around the world. A quick look at market shares of tourism among different regions (WTO statistics 2007) can give us a clear idea about this growth and about the relationship between globalization and tourism. Since the year 1995, the number of tourists' arrivals has been increasing till it reached the total of 842 million international tourists (about 36 million tourists more), with an average increase of 4.5% yearly .This increase of the 36 millions tourists was distributed over tourism regions as follows: Europe (17 millions: 47%), Asia and Pacific (12 millions: 33%), Americas (3 millions: 8%), Africa (3 millions: 8%), and Middle East (1.5 million: 4%) (WTO 2007). Such distribution of increase in tourists' numbers was to continue, the distribution of tourists' arrivals in 2009 is reflecting the significant differences among world regions' shares in term of both arrivals and receipts .Such distribution of tourists' arrivals among different world regions is indicating a very serious issue; some of these regions are considerably higher than others in terms of the market share they hold. First World countries are receiving the bulk of international tourists, consequently are receiving most of the revenues from them; that is in addition to the fact that they can generate more income per international tourist than third World countries, therefore, a reality of globalization is to be seen here characterized by the uneven and unequal development, simply justified by the level of tourism development and facilities provided in their destinations Some countries are becoming integrated into the global economy more quickly than others, leaving other countries with declined economies, poverty increased in them and high inflation became their norm (IMF 2000). Considering the great role of tourism in supporting economies, it is not unusual then to be perceived by cash-starved Third World countries as a shortcut to rapid development. Many of these countries found the Structural Adjustment Program (SAPs) offered by International Monetary Fund (IMF) to be the solution to their deteriorating economic situations since it offers financial assistance. The SAPs, which are preconditions for the approval of financial assistance, require the indebted country to be integrated into the global economy; deregulate and liberalize its economy; shift from an agriculture-based to a manufacturing and service industry-based economy; and liberalize its financial sector. The strategy of SAP is based on involving countries' economies in foreign investments and multinational corporations, while eliminating subsidies and protection to local industries. With the great power of tourism as income and employment generator, the Third World governments tried to fulfill these conditions through establishing infrastructure projects such as roads, hotels and tourist-promotion programs, also increasing the opportunities for more international investments to take place in their lands. Worldwide, public and private investments have reached $800 billion annually, accounting for 12% of total worldwide investments (Chavez 1999). Such revolution in the economy of these countries and development of tourism, all resulted in the increase of tourism destinations numbers; consequently, the tourism market became and is still becoming increasingly segmented into different kinds of tourism markets and preferences instead of mass tourism (Mowforth & Munt 2003). Such markets included ecotourism in destinations as parks, nature reserves, and natural settings; cultural and heritage tourism in different historic and cultural sites and experiencing customs and lifestyles, as well as folklore of different communities; adventure tourism as in mountain climbing, scuba-diving and walking along park trails; health tourism in natural hot springs, sport tourism as World Cup football and Olympic events; and cruise ships sailing from different ports around the world By noticing that many of the destinations (in which some of these forms of tourism are taking place) are in developing countries; and considering that tourism in these countries has been increasing annually by 6% as compared to 3.5% in developed countries, and the fact that they include a big number of undisturbed environments and the majority of the distinct indigenous cultures; all these issues make them became a target of globalized economies and crowds of tourists (Chavez 1999); mainly from First World (developed countries). Despite all these facts, these Third World countries still cannot receive the same amounts of profits First World countries make out of tourism (Mowforth & Munt 2003). The increase of tourism in Third World countries might have resulted in an economic benefit through the numbers of arrivals and profits, but it had also its negative impact on their environments and communities, of which Arab countries located in the two regions of Middle East and North Africa, are forming a significant part.

Why is Tourism Important to Arab Countries?

Tourism is considered as a major source of foreign exchange, being then important to Arab countries' economy for balance-of-trade purposes and the development of infrastructure (e.g. in Jordan, tourism is considered as the main source of foreign exchange earnings after the remittances from overseas Jordanian workers). Tourism also is a crucial generator of employment to many of these countries (e.g. according to the Egyptian Tourism Authority, 10% of the Egyptian population is depending on tourism for earning their living, of which a significant proportion is of semi-skilled and unskilled employees; in Bahrain, 17-18% of Jobs are in tourism, either directly or indirectly; in Oman, hotels are required by law to have 50% of its employees from local national employees). Tourism also helps in reducing the dependence on other sources of economy (e.g. Gulf countries are giving a very good example here, these countries have started to recognize the importance of tourism to decrease their reliance on oil revenues in the long term, e.g. Dubai in UAE, Oman, Qatar and Bahrain); though, some other countries with big oil reserves are slow toward tourism development, that is due to the lack of need to diversify their economies (as Abu Dhabi in UAE, Kuwait and Saudi Arabia) (WTO 2003).

According to the reports of World Travel and Tourism Council, the economic activities are indicating a more promising contribution of tourism and travel industry to Arab countries economies. In 2009, travel & tourism is expected to post US$241.9 billions of economic activity (as a total demand), growing to US$529.8 billion by 2019 in the Middle East region (WTTC 2009a). This also can be seen to what regards the contribution to world GDP, the travel and tourism industry is expected to post a GDP contribution of 3.9% in 2009 (WTTC 2009 a & b). Middle East travel and tourism employment is expected to generate 5,130,000 jobs in 2009, 9.0% of total employment, or 1 in every 11.1 jobs. By 2019, this total is predicted to become 6,876,000 jobs, 9.5% of total employment or 1 in every 10.5 jobs (WTTC 2009a).

In North Africa, travel & tourism is expected to post US$78.8 billions of economic activity (as a total demand), growing to US$158.7 billion by 2019 (WTTC 2009b). North Africa travel and tourism employment is estimated to become 5,440,000 jobs in 2009, 11.2% of total employment, or 1 in every 8.9 jobs. By 2019, this number of jobs is expected to end with 6,914,000 jobs, 11.3% of total employment or 1 in every 8.8 jobs (WTTC 2009b).

Considering the vital role of travel and tourism as a major exporter, since inbound visitors inject foreign exchange directly into the economy; of total Middle East exports, travel and tourism is expected to generate 13.4% (US$100.1 billion) in 2009, increasing to US$226.8 billion (12.4% of total) in 2019. The Middle East's travel and tourism industry is expected to contribute 2.7% to Gross Domestic Product (GDP) in 2009 (US$44.4 billion), rising to US$100.8 billion (2.7% of total) by 2019. Middle East travel and tourism capital investment is estimated at US$47.0 billion or 11.9% of total investment in year 2009. By 2019, this estimate is expected to reach US$82.9 billion or 10.2% of total (WTTC 2009a). In North Africa, total exports of travel and tourism is expected to generate 18.1% (US$35.1 billion) in 2009, increasing to US$70.8 billion (15.4% of total), in 2019. North Africa's travel and tourism industry is expected to contribute 5.3% to Gross Domestic Product (GDP) in 2009 (US$29.6 billion), rising to become US$55.5 billion (5.2% of total) by 2019. In North Africa, travel and tourism capital investment is estimated to be US$14.2 billion or 10.7% of total investment in year 2009, this estimate is predicted to reach US$27.7billions or 10.8% of total by 2019 (WTTC 2009b).

Growth of Tourism in Arab World

There are several potentials that make the growth of tourism in the Arab countries promising; for international tourism: being close enough to the inclusive tour markets of north-west Europe (the main generator of tourists), which have tourism based mainly on sun, sea and sand; extensive tourism infrastructure as good roads and airports of an international standards; that is in addition to the considerable hotel development in major cities and coastal resorts; being in the crossroads between Europe, Africa and Asia, consequently forming good staging points for businesses on the long routes between Western Europe and the East Asia Pacific regions; the richness in cultural attractions (archaeological, historical and religious sites) since the region occupied the earliest civilizations and the three major world religions (Judaism, Christianity and Islam); the favorable climate for beach tourism and the increase in resorts, the opportunities for some winter sports in some mountain ranges (Binoface & Cooper 2001). For intraregional tourism (tourism from Arab countries) an increase is expected due to: the close similarity in customs and traditions as well as a common language, the limited need for require heavy outlay on infrastructure as hotels since the majority of Arab tourists travel with their families and prefer accommodation in family housing and furnished flats; being enforced with the fact that family connections and intermarriage between nationals of different Arab countries create 'intraregional extended families'; the ease in dealing with airports, hotels and shops because of the common language; variety in history, civilization, climate and temperature; the growth of new tourism trends as 'medical tourism' between Arab countries (as in the case of Jordan, which hosts a number of visitors from Iraq, the Libyan Arab Jamahiriya, the Syrian Arab Republic and Yemen), also educational tourism (the big numbers of Arab students studying at Arab universities especially after 11 September 2001) (ESCWA 2007). The Middle East for example is considered to be one of the fastest growing global destinations; a considerable growth in terms of tourism facilities is witnessed (e.g. Intercontinental Hotels has announced it will open 20 Holiday Inns, Easy Group has confirmed it will bring 38 hotels to the region by 2011) (APN 2007). Till the last few decades, the availability of oil in some countries as in the case of Gulf States eliminated the need to diversify their economies because of such prosperity. Later, these countries became aware that such source will be soon exhausted, and so they started to attract tourism development to diversify their economic base (as in the case of Dubai Commerce and Tourism Promotion Board, which is using its oil wealth to create golf courses in the desert to become a cruise destination) (Boniface & Cooper 2001). Despite this strong need for tourism, there are some obstacles facing its development, especially on the intraregional scale; these are: weak Arab cooperation in tourism, lack of regular flights, the inadequate provision of tourism products (although of their diversity), moreover, the disability to provide tourism services in an adequate manner (ESCWA 2007). Not less important to the previous factors is the unstable political situation in the region (i.e. Palestinian-Israeli conflict, Gulf War 1990-1 ...etc), the lack of management and capacity to receive visitors at some sites, the lack of awareness in some segments of Arab societies about the importance of tourism and its benefits, causing then a negative perception and reaction toward tourism (particularly from a socio-cultural point of view), a situation that generates a number of calamities in some regions (i.e. kidnapping of western tourists by tribesmen in the interior highlands of Yemen, terrorism attacks on tourists during 1990s in Egypt) (Boniface & Cooper 2001). This case was to continue after a number of international crises which affected the growth of tourism worldwide and in Arab countries as well (e.g. Iraq War started in 2003, and the spread of some diseases as SARS) (WTO 2004b).

Globalization Effect on Arab Countries through Tourism

In addition to the strengths mentioned above, some other factors influencing the growth of tourism worldwide (economically and technologically wise) under the name of 'Globalization' are supporting this industry in Arab countries; these include the improvement of access to these countries by the development of transportation and its infrastructure; the increase in investment incentives; improvement and diversification of tourism products; the enhancement of marketing activities (by quality and quantity); the institutional development; the public-private partnership taking place now in many countries; the improvement of electronic technology (for getting the information and buying the trip); the emerge of new meanings in the experience of tourism (the 3 E's: Entertainment, Excitement, and Education) among wide segments of societies (particularly Arab societies) and witnessing the destination as a fashion accessory (WTO 2004a). In a report published by Wells (2004), it was mentioned that many destinations in the Middle East region were having an increase in tourism arrivals for the years 2003 and 2004; which is resulting from development of the intra-regional market; moreover, the tourists from western and southern Europe. Egypt witnessed a significant increase in the number of visitors that reached 49% up to August 2003, while receipts increased by 52% in the first half of the same year. Some countries had some considerable risings in their arrival numbers; according to WTO, about 42% more tourists from the Arab market up to July 2004 were recorded in Lebanon, while the total number grew by an estimate of 30%. About 60% increase in total arrivals, with a 70% rise in inter-Arab trade was observed in Syria. Other destinations such as Dubai (+9%), Bahrain (+19%) and Jordan (+18%) also benefited from the strong world demand. The ascending numbers of international arrivals to the North African destinations was noticed as well, an increase of 19% in Tunisia and 17% in Morocco were recorded for the year 2004, tourism receipts were also growing (+3% in Morocco and +15% in Tunisia up to June 2004). According to the information of WTO (2000-2003), some of the Arab countries were having a big share from the total number of tourists coming to the Middle East and North African countries; this was noticed in countries like Saudi Arabia depending on pilgrimage seasons (7,511 million tourists for 2002), Egypt with the great number of ancient Egyptian sites, coastal resorts and Nile tours (5,745 million tourists for 2003), Morocco with its richness of historical sites and coastal resorts (4,552 million tourists for 2003), UAE because of its huge investments and shopping events (5,445 million tourists for 2002), Tunisia with its main attractions of coastal resorts and historical sites (5,153 million tourists for 2003), Bahrain attracting tourists for its heritage houses and shopping (3,167 million tourists for 2002), and Syria with its historical sites and different resorts (2,809 million tourists for 2002). These countries then are followed by other countries that occupy a variety of attractions in their small areas as Jordan (1,573 million tourists for 2003) and Lebanon (1,016 million tourists for 2003). Some other countries though were slow toward tourism development and promotion, either because of diversification in their economy (as in the case of Kuwait, Oman and Qatar), or mainly because of lack in development and promotion of their tourism sites, as well as unstable political or social situations (as in the case of Yemen and Iraq) (WTO 2003). This growth though was not to continue, the statistics given by WTO (2007) about the increase percentages within the years (2005/4 & 2006/5) shows a general decrease that took place in most of world regions; such decrease though was noticed to be slight in regions as Africa, Asia Pacific and Europe; while at regions as the Americas and Middle east, such decrease was higher by comparison . The Numbers of Tourists' Arrivals within (2000-2003) Among Arab Countries (WTO 2004a) The Percentage of Increase in the Number of Tourists within (2005-2006) Among Tourism Regions (WTO 2007) For Arab countries, the statistics show that Middle East had only an increase of (3.9% for 2006/5) compared to (8.4% for 2005/4); the same applies to North Africa, where an increase of only (5.8% for 2006/5) compared to (8.9% for 2005/4) is recorded. Such numbers are somehow reflecting the reality of a situation, which is about the continuous unequal benefits among world regions due to the case of uneven development and stability, an issue that is related to globalization, since it reflects the economic, political and technological dominance that is constrained only to some developed countries and powers, this is to seen also by looking at WTO statistics for the years 2008 and 2009.

The impacts of tourism that are perceived by and affecting residents of any destination take many forms. The economic impacts of tourism are seen through enhancing income and living standards (Pizam 1978), providing jobs opportunities (Liu & Var 1986; Milman & Pizam 1988), increasing investment, increasing tax revenues, and improving the infrastructure (Milman & Pizam 1988), though, tourism contributes to the increase of prices of lands and properties as well as the prices of goods and services (Liu & Var 1986; Pizam 1978). Environment wise, tourism supports the protection of natural areas as well as the preservation of historic heritage and buildings (Liu & Var 1987, Sethna & Richmond 1978), on the other hand, tourism can increase congestion and crowding, besides contributing to different types of pollution (Pizam 1978). Socio cultural impacts of tourism are characterized by the improvement of life quality (Pizam 1978), contribution to cultural exchange and understanding among different committees and their meeting together; moreover, it helps in preserving the cultural identity of host culture. In some cases, tourism contributed to the spread of some negative values as prostitution, smuggling, alcoholism (Liu & Var 1987). Tourism influence on locals' way of life and on their control of and access to their resources has become very obvious with the globalization of world economy. It is already seen in many regions worldwide that tourism had brought long-term damaging effects on some local communities, even prior to globalization. Even with the case of local communities, which are still unaffected by traditional tourism activities, they have now been targeted for tourism ventures, more particularly, ecotourism and other kinds of new tourism (Chavez 1999). This is simply due to the pace of tourism development, increase in the number of tourists and the competition of tourism with other economic sectors. As Hazbun (1997) states, getting the economic benefits of tourism by Arab countries requires some tradeoffs, which include foregoing investments in other sectors, environmental degradation, social segregation and privatization of public space.

All of the mentioned above impacts initiate the need to have a very carefully managed and planned tourism, which aims mainly at the economic, social and environmental sustainability in any region. Although of the positive aspects of tourism in Arab countries; negative impacts were not discussed in many studies, reflecting then a lack of awareness about future threats to locals and environments, as well as a lack in implementing measures and indicators to monitor the condition of resources and sites exposed to tourism development.

The problems of tourism in Arab countries were mentioned in few studies; of which some were dealing with environmental degradation as air pollution, inappropriate disposal of solid waste, the untreated wastewater discharged to the sea and so contaminating ground water, using great amounts of detergents and chemicals by hotels, the damage of coral reefs by tourists to keep them as souvenirs, and the disturbance of wildlife in the Red Sea area in Egypt (Shaalan 2005); the conflict between tourists and pilgrims because of contradiction in beliefs (the case of Baha'i Gardens in Haifa (Gatrell & Kreiner 2006); the social and environmental deterioration and the clash between Islamic and European values in Tunisia (Poirier 1995); the cross border competition in gambling tourism between Israel and Egypt and its negative impact on societies (Felsenstein & Freeman 2001); the result of development pressure by tourism, which is characterized by the over exploitation of the natural resource base of the fragile region (as in the case of Mount Sinai and the Monastery of Saint Katherine in Egypt) (Grainger 2003); the harassment of tourists by false guides, dropping of schools by students to work in tourism, excluding locals from some areas as beaches, and pollution of coasts and sea water in Tunisia, terrorism against tourists in Egypt (Hazbun 1997). All of these studies and some others are indicating warning signs against the deterioration of environments and segregation of communities, which are caused by the growth of tourism supported by globalization aspects. It becomes clear that globalization and tourism are generating a considerable benefit to many communities and countries through their relationship. The significant increase seen in the number of tourists' arrivals and revenues is with no doubt a main target for any tourism development; but issues as the quality of environmental resources, biodiversity, and the respect of local communities should be also considered. The economic benefits are always focused on and evaluated with different kinds of variables and measures. The problem is that such concern is not equally given to the environmental and social issues, initiating then the need to have more sustainable approach in tourism development planning by formal authorities and other stakeholders. More coordination between Arab tourism authorities would support the expansion of tourist numbers, though it should be combined with improvement of tourist services besides controlling their performance to avoid any deterioration in the authenticity of cultures or environmental resources.

According to WTO & UNEP (2005), some policy areas if taken into account would be the approach to achieve sustainability in tourism; these include: ensuring the viability and competitiveness of tourism destinations and enterprises by understanding what potential consumers are looking for; and adapt to trends and changes in source market conditions, as well as travel patterns and tastes, this requires an effective and ongoing market research; maximizing the contribution of tourism to the economic prosperity of the host destination by supporting locally owned businesses, and ensuring employment of local labor; ensuring a widespread and fair distribution of economic and social benefits from tourism throughout the recipient community, including improving opportunities, income and services available to the poor; engaging the local community in the development of tourism policies and plans; in addition to respecting and enhancing the historic heritage, authentic culture, traditions and distinctiveness of host communities, maintain and enhance the quality of landscapes, both urban and rural, and avoid the physical and visual degradation of the environment.

References

1. Allen, J. & Massey, D. 1995. Geographical Worlds, Open University Press, Milton Keynes. APN. 2007. Middle East Forecast to Grow 7% a Year, Asia Pulse News, on the date: 02.12.2007.
2. Boniface, B. & Cooper, C. 2001. Worldwide Destinations: The Geography of Travel and Tourism, 3rd edition, Butterworth-Heinemann, Oxford.
3. Chavez, R. 1999. Globalization and Tourism: Deadly Mix for Indigenous Peoples, Third World Resurgence No. 103. *International Journal of Business and Social Science Vol. 1 No. 1; October 2010*
4. Cogburn, D. 1998. Globalization, Knowledge, Education and Training in the Global World, Conference Paper for the Info Ethics 98, UNESCO.
5. ESCWA. 2007. The Annual Review of Developments in Globalization and Regional Integration in the Arab Countries, issued by Economic and Social Commission for Western Asia, United Nations, New York.
6. Felsenstein, D. & Freeman, D. 2001. Estimating the Impacts of Cross-border Competition: the Case of Gambling in Israel and Egypt, Tourism Management, 22(5): 511-521.
7. Gatrell, J. & Kreiner, N. 2006. Negotiated Space: Tourists, Pilgrims, and the Bahá'í Terraced Gardens in Haifa, Geoforum, 37(5), 765-778.
8. Gee, Chunk Y. 1997. International Tourism: A Global Prospective; World Tourism Organization.
9. Grainger, J. 2003. People are Living in the Park'. Linking Biodiversity Conservation to Community Development in the Middle East Region: a Case Study from the Saint Katherine Protectorate, Southern Sinai, Journal of Arid Environments, 54: 29–38.
10. Hall, S. 1992. The Question of Cultural Identity, in Modernity and its Future, edited by S. Hall, D. Held and T. McGrew, Polity Press, Oxford.

11. Hazbun, W. 1997. The Development of Tourism Industries in the Arab World: Trapped Between the Forces of Economic Globalization and Cultural Commodification, an expanded version of a paper presented at 30th Annual Convention of the Association of Arab-American University Graduates (AAUG) on the theme of "Arabs, Arab Americans & the Global Community" November 1, 1997 in Washington, DC.
12. Hawkins, D. & Lamoureux, K. 2001. Global Growth and Magnitude of Ecotourism, in the Encyclopedia of Ecotourism, edited by D. Weaver, 63-72, CABI Publishing, Wallingford.
13. Held, D., McGrew, A., Goldblatt, D. & Perraton, J. 1999. Global Transformations - Politics, Economics and Culture, Cambridge: Polity Press.
14. IMF. 2000. Globalization: Threat or Opportunity, A Report by the Staff of International Monetary Fund,
15. (January 2002).
16. ILO. 2001. Human Resources Development, Employment and Globalization in the Hotel, Catering and Tourism Sector, Report for discussion at the Tripartite Meeting on the Human Resources Development, Employment and Globalization in the Hotel, Catering and Tourism Sector, International Labor Organization Office, Geneva.
17. IVC. 2006. The Economic Impact of Air Service Liberalization, Inter Vistas- Consulting, Inc.: http//: www.intervistas.us.
18. Liu, J. & Var, T. 1986. Resident Attitudes toward Tourism Impacts in Hawaii. Annals of Tourism Research, 13 (2): 193-214.
19. Milman, A., and Pizam, A. 1988. Social Impacts of Tourism on Central Florida, Annals of Tourism Research, 15 (2): 191-204.
20. Mowforth, M. & Munt, I. 2003. Tourism and Sustainability, 2nd edition, London: Routledge.
21. Pizam, A. 1978. Tourist Impacts: The Social Costs to the Destination Community as Perceived by its

22. Residents. *Journal of Travel Research,* 16(4), 8-12. *Centre for Promoting Ideas, USA*
23. Poirier, R. 1995. Tourism and Development in Tunisia, Annals of Tourism Research, 22(1), 157-171.
24. Scholte, J. 2000. Globalization. A Critical Introduction, London: Palgrave.
25. Scholte, J. 1997. Global Capitalism and the State, International Affairs, 73(3), 427-452.
26. Sethna, R. J., and Richmond, B.1978. U.S. Virgin Islanders' Perceptions of Tourism. Journal of Travel Research, 17: 30-31.
27. UNESCO. 1999. Tourism and Culture: Rethinking the Mix, the UNESCO Courier, (July-August issue): 21- 56.
28. Vogeler, C. 2010. World Tourism: 2009 & Beyond; a Presentation given at Tourism Out Look Seminar:
29. Challenges, Changes and Opportunities in Tourism, Rising above the Current Global Economic Landscape (2-3 February 2010), Montego Bay.
30. Wells, R. 2004. World Travel Market Highlights Middle East Tourism: Special Report, the Middle East, published on the date: 12/01/2004.
31. WTO. 2003. Inbound Tourism to Middle East and North Africa, World Tourism Organization.
32. WTO. 2004a. Tourism 2020 Vision: The Challenges and Opportunities for Middle East Destinations, a presentation by A. Abdel-Ghaffar (a regional representative of WTO for the Middle East) in a seminar on ETourism: The Route to Competitive Success, Damascus, Syria (April 27th & 28th 2004).
33. WTO. 2004b. International and European Tourism: 2003 and beyond, a presentation by: L. Cabrini (a
34. regional representative of WTO for Europe) in a seminar for the Regional Commission for Europe, 42nd meeting, Rimini and San Marino, Italy, May 2004, 19-21.
35. WTO. 2007. Barometer (Issue of June 2007), Volume 5(2), World Tourism Organization: http://www.unwto.org.

36. WTO. 2010. Barometer (Issue of June 2010), Volume 8 (2), World Tourism Organization: http://www.unwto.org

Chapter 8
Globalization and Environment

Economic globalization impacts the environment and sustainable development in a wide variety of ways and through a multitude of channels. The purpose of this chapter is (a) to identify the key links between globalization and environment; (b) to identify the major issues addressed in multilateral economic agreements in trade and finance that affect environmental sustainability; and (c) to review priority policy issues affecting the environment in multilateral economic agreements and environment, thus identifying incentives implicit in trade and investment policy measures that affect environmental sustainability. The author categorizes these issues under the primary areas of globalization: trade liberalization, investment and finance, and technology diffusion, the latter including intellectual property rights. In the case of the trade-environment interface, the unit examines the impact of both elements, and the causal relationship between them. It also pays special attention to multilateral environmental agreements and their potential effects on trade. An integrative section on the effects of globalization and environmental policy and performance leads to domestic and international priority policy issues and recommendations. The author concludes that globalization brings with it potentially large benefits as well as risks. The challenge is to manage the process of globalization in such a way that it promotes environmental sustainability and equitable human development. In short, the more integrated environmental and trade policies are, the more sustainable economic growth will be and the more globalization can be harnessed for the benefit of the environment. globalization has been the defining trend in the closing decade of the 20th century and the dawn of new millennium heralding a new era of interaction among nations, economies and people. Globalization is an on-going process of global integration that encompasses (i) economic integration through trade, investment and capital flows; (ii) political interaction; (iii) information and information technology and (iv) culture. While all dimensions of globalization affect the natural environment and through it human development, for the purposes of tracing the main lines between globalization and environment we will focus on the economic dimensions of trade, investment and capital flows. An unprecedented flow of capital, technology, goods and services crosses national borders daily. Nearly 20 billion US dollars in capital flows around the world each day.

Economic globalization impacts the environment and sustainable development in a variety of ways and through a multitude of channels. Globalization contributes to economic growth and thereby affects the environment in many of the same ways that economic growth does: adversely in some stages of development, favorably at others. Globalization accelerates structural change, thereby altering the industrial structure of countries and hence resource use and pollution levels. Globalization diffuses capital and technology; depending on their environmental characteristics relative to existing capital and technology, the environment may improve or deteriorate. Globalization transmits and magnifies market failures and policy distortions that may spread and exacerbate environmental damage; it may also generate pressures for reform as policies heretofore thought of as purely domestic attract international interest. While it improves the prospects for economic growth worldwide and increases overall global output, globalization could conceivably reduce economic prospects in individual countries, sectors and industries; such marginalization of economies and people may result in poverty-induced resource depletion and environmental degradation.

Globalization diffuses world product standards and, to the extent that environmental standards are higher in the dominant consumer markets, it may create a trend toward rising standards globally; on the other hand, concerns over the possible loss of competitiveness due to "unfair practices" or lax standards may lead to a "race to the bottom." Economic globalization changes the government-market interface; it constraints governments and enhances the role of the market in economic, social and environmental outcomes; on the other hand, it creates new imperatives for states to co-operate both in managing the global commons and in coordinating domestic environmental policies.

The purpose of this topic is to (a) identify the key links between globalization and environment; (b) identify major issues included in multilateral economic agreements in trade, finance, investments and intellectual property rights that affect environmental sustainability; and (c) review priority policy issues affecting multilateral economic agreements and environment, to analyze incentives implicit in trade and investment policy measures that affect environmental sustainability. Since this a vast area to cover, we have divided it into the main dimensions of economic globalization: trade liberalization, investment and finance and technology diffusion and intellectual property rights. In the case of the trade-environment interface, we consider both the impact of trade on the environment and of the environment on trade. An integrative section on the effects of globalization on the environmental policy and performance leads to domestic and international priority policy issues and recommendations.

Trade and Environment

Trade liberalization and its outcome, freer trade, are both drivers and manifestations of globalization. They are also major channels through which globalization impacts the natural environment and affects environmental quality. World trade has grown faster than world output indicating a growing trade-intensity of the global economy. While global output grew at an average annual rate of 4% during 1950-94, the world merchandise trade grew at an average annual rate of over 6% during the same period. As a result, over the 45 year period, world merchandise trade grew by 14 times compared to only 5.5 times for the world merchandise output. The trade intensity of the global economy increased further during 1990-1995 (WTO 1995).

Trade theory has demonstrated that free trade maximizes the efficiency of resource allocation by channeling economic activities to least-cost producers; it thus produces a given level of output at the least cost. If natural and environmental resources are efficiently priced (i.e. all relevant social costs are accounted for), the global output resulting from free trade is also produced at the least environmental cost. Free trade maximizes social welfare. For example, countries with high levels of agricultural protection use more than ten times as much chemical fertilizers and pesticides per hectare as countries with low level protection. In this case, trade liberalization would reduce the use of agrochemicals and hence environmental degradation in protectionist countries significantly and increase it marginally in low protection countries resulting in overall gains in environmental protection and sustainability. If, however, there are market failures (such as unpriced or underpriced resources or unaccounted for externalities), or policy failures (such as environmentally-harmful subsidies) that are not removed, resources are misallocated to start with and removal of barriers to trade may exacerbate this misallocation. Under such conditions, freer trade would not maximize social welfare. There would still be efficiency gains (positive effects) but there would also be welfare losses as wasteful resource depletion and environmental degradation are exacerbated (negative effects). The net effect on social welfare would depend on the relative magnitude of the positive and negative effects. There are few studies attempting to estimate and compare the efficiency gains from trade liberalization with the costs of increased environmental degradation or needed additional environmental protection measures. Repetto (1993) attempted such a comparison and concluded that there is no *a priori* case for giving trade policy a priority over environmental policy. Efficiency gains from trade liberalization were estimated to range from 1 - 2 percent of GDP to 3- 4 percent for economies with severe economic distortions. Environmental control costs and residual environmental damage costs, on the other hand, range from 1 - 2 percent of GDP to 3 - 5 percent of GDP in countries with lax environmental policies.

Trade-related Environmental Effects

1. Scale effects — negative effects, when increased trade leads to more pollution without compensating product, technology or policy developments; positive effects, when increased trade induces better environmental protection through economic growth and policy development that stimulates product composition and technology shifts that cause less pollution per unit of output.
2. Structural effects — changes in the patterns of economic activity or micro-economic production, consumption, investment, or geographic effects from increased trade that either exert positive environmental effects, (e.g. reducing production of crops that rely on chemical intensive methods, in favor of more extensive agriculture), or cause negative consequences (e.g. encouraging the drainage of wetlands to satisfy new trade demands).
3. Income effects — positive effects increased willingness to pay with increased personal incomes brought about by growth-induced trade; also increased budgetary resources allocated to environmental protection both in absolute and relative terms.
4. Product effects — either positive effects, from increased trade in goods that are environmentally beneficial, e.g. biodegradable containers, or negative effects, from more trade in environmentally damaging products, e.g. hazardous wastes.

5. Technology effects — either positive effects from reducing pollution per unit of product, e.g., precision farming that reduces excess fertilizer use, or negative effects from the spread of "dirty" technologies, e.g., highly toxic and persistent pesticides, through trade channels.

6. Regulatory effects — either through improved environmental policies, in response to economic growth from enhanced trade or through measures included in the trade agreement, or the relaxation of existing environmental policies, because of specific trade pressures or restrictions on environmental policy by trade agreements. To better understand how globalization-induced free trade impacts the environment, it is necessary to examine the channels through which such impacts are transmitted. There are six such channels: (a) scale of economic activity; (b) income growth; (c) changes in structure of economic activity; (d) product composition; (e) technology diffusion; and (f) trade-induced regulations. (See Box 1 for a summary of these effects).

Scale effects

To the extent that trade liberalization stimulates economic growth, both the scale of economic activity and incomes increase. A larger volume of economic activity would certainly raise the aggregate level of natural resource use and environmental pollution unless improved resource efficiency and structural change reduce resource use and pollution intensity per unit of output more than proportionally. For given structure and resource use efficiency, the scale effects on the environment of trade liberalization are unambiguously negative. Negative scale effects are more pronounced where there are market failures such as ill defined property rights, un priced ecosystems, uninternalized externalities and underprovided public goods. Policy failures such as energy subsidies or forced industrialization further exacerbate the scale effects of trade liberalization. Income effects

The gains from trade and trade-induced economic growth result in substantial income increases which impact the environment in a variety of ways. First, higher incomes result in both higher levels of consumption and associated environmental externalities, and in higher willingness to pay for environmental improvement, and associated increases in both private and public environmental expenditures. There is considerable empirical evidence that environmental quality is income elastic, in the sense that increases in income result in more than proportionate increases in environmental expenditures. Second, economic growth makes more resources available for environmental protection, and raises environmental quality in a country's list of priorities, prompting governments to increase environmental expenditures both in absolute terms and as a percentage of GDP. This is true of virtually all the newly industrializing countries (from China and South Korea to Mexico and Brazil). The reverse is also true, when income growth slows down (as after the recent Asian financial crisis), environmental expenditures tend to fall more than proportionally.

Third, to the extent that trade and growth benefits are widely distributed, trade liberalization may help reduce the pressures placed by poverty on the environment through the encroachment of natural resources. If, on the other hand, poor people (either rural or urban) are further marginalized by global competition without access to technology, capital and other means to compete, encroachment and degradation of natural resources (forest, pastures, fisheries, public lands) are likely to intensify. Trade liberalization may actually reinforce the vicious circle between poverty and environmental degradation, especially when open access resources, heretofore poor people's last resort source of livelihood, are now being exploited for exports. Ironically, economic collapse may not reduce the pressure on natural resources, if impoverished urban dwellers return to the rural areas reclaiming their traditional sources of livelihood as indeed happened in Thailand and Indonesia following the recent financial crisis. Finally, economic growth may result in reform of environmental policies and enactment of new laws and regulations and new institutions to enforce them. Studies of the relationship between income levels and environmental degradation, not controlling for scale and structural change effects, found an inverted U-shape relationship, especially for localized effects. (Grossman and Krueger, 1995, Panayotou 1997a). At low-income levels (early stages of development), income growth is associated with higher levels of environmental degradation until a turning point is reached (between US$5,000-10,000) beyond which further income increases result in environmental improvement. This finding came to be known as the Environmental Kuznets Curve, tends to suggest that environmental degradation is a "growing up" problem to be overcome through rapid economic growth rather than through targeted environmental policies. To the extent that free trade speeds up economic growth and raises per capita incomes, any restrictions on trade or diversions of resources away from exported growth slow down the transition to a positive income-environment relationship. This is clearly a misinterpretation of an empirical relationship that is devoid of policy significance in its reduced form. First, it ignores the role of market and policy failures in determining the level of environmental damage cost per additional unit of GDP, and the scope for policy reform to reduce it. Second, it ignores threshold effects and the risk of irreversible environmental damages was environmental degradation to cross such thresholds before reaching the turning point. Third, current income levels of developing countries are nowhere close to the turning point, hence environment-intensive production would continue for a long time, resulting in significant and possibly irreversible environmental damage. Policy formulation calls for a more analytical and disaggregated approach to the income environment relationship. Once such attempt (Panayotou 1997a) decomposed the income environment relationship into: (a) a scale effect which was found to be unambiguously negative; (b) a pure income effect which was found to be unambiguously positive, and a composition or structural change effect which was found to be negative at earlier stages of development (shift from agriculture into industry) and positive at later stages of development (shift from industry to services). The speed of income growth was also found to matter, resulting in somewhat higher levels of environmental degradation per unit of GDP. However, it was also found that effective policy intervention is a potent means to reducing the environmental cost of growth at all stages of economic development. Thus, while some deterioration of environmental quality is inevitable along a country's development path up to the turning point, policy interventions to remove distortions and mitigate market failures can reduce the environmental cost of growth and hence of trade and keep it at reversible levels below critical ecological thresholds.

Structural or Composition Effects

Globalization in general and freer trade in particular results in a shift in industrial structure more in line with a country's comparative advantage. In the absence of market and policy failures, the composition of output under free trade would be better suited to a country's environmental resource endowment than under austerity. Controlling for scale effects and for stage of development, trade liberalization tends to make the structure of the economy less pollution-intensive to speed up the transition from resource extraction and processing to light manufacturing and eventually services. Since most developing countries are more richly endowed in low-cost labor than any other factor of production, trade liberalization tends to shift labor-intensive activities to developing countries. Indeed, Hettige, Lucas and Wheeler (1992) found that toxic intensity increased more rapidly in inward-looking developing countries, while outward-oriented, high-growth developing countries had a slowly increasing or declining toxic intensity of manufacturing. They found that highly protected economies had experienced rapid growth in capital-intensive smokestack sectors, while more open economies had experienced high growth in less pollution-intensive, more labor-intensive activities. Developing countries may also have significant national resource endowments and income-constrained demand for environmental quality. The extent to which trade liberalization would contribute to sustainable development, under these conditions, depends critically on whether environmental assets are properly valued, and these values are somehow been taken into account by world markets. Otherwise, trade liberalization may result in structural shifts towards increased specialization in unsustainable activities. A recent study by Strutt and Anderson (1998), however, found that, even under business as usual scenario (i.e., no change in resource pricing or environmental regulation), implementation of the Uruguay Round trade reforms would have a positive impact on natural resource in developing countries and most other regimes of the world except for Western Europe where resource policies are well developed and can cope with any increase in resource exploitation.

Product and Technology Effects

Liberalized trade facilitates the diffusion of products, technologies and processes across borders. The environmental impacts of this diffusion depend on the characteristics of the products and technologies that are being diffused. The trade in products that are patently harmful to the environment such as toxic chemicals, hazardous waste, endangered species and disease bearing pests is strictly regulated or prohibited by international conventions. A very important channel through which globalization impacts the environment is the trade in environmentally preferred "producer" and "consumer" goods. The global market for environmental goods and services is around $300 billion annually and is expected to grow rapidly (OECD 1996). Trade liberalization expands the potential market for both more efficient capital equipment and "cleaner" production technologies on the production side and "greener" products, such as organic foods, low-emission vehicles and recyclables, on the consumption side. While other dimensions of globalization, such as investment, intellectual property rights and economic integration have technology implications that impact the environment, three quarters of all technology transfer arise from trade flows (OECD 1995), especially the trade in machinery and equipment, which amounts to almost

40 percent of total global trade (UN 1996). These trade flows result in diffusion of more efficient (and one hopes cleaner) technologies: almost 80 percent of the global trade in machinery and equipment comes from developed countries and about a third is imported by developing countries (UN 1996). Technology diffusion also takes place through the trade in services such as engineering and consulting services and technology licensing. \Liberalized trade contributes not only to technology diffusion and transfer but also to technological progress through economies of scale, enhanced incentives to innovate and less duplication of research and development efforts due to fewer protectionist barriers (Grossman and Helpman 1995). Does the trade-induced generation and diffusion of technology benefits or harms the environment? The technology-environment relationship is a complex one consisting of both demand and supply factors and policy effects. On the demand side, pressures by regulators, customers, shareholders and the community drive firms to demand technology with environmental characteristics such as "cleaner" production technology and pollution-abatement equipment. While regulatory and community pressures usually aim at process characteristics, customers pressure is directed towards product characteristics. Studies of firm behavior in developed countries tend to find regulatory pressure as the most potent driver of environmentally-preferred technologies (e.g. Henriques and Sadorsky,1996) while studies of firm behavior in developing countries tend to find community pressures as the most important determinant of firms' environmental behavior (Pargal and Wheeler, 1995; Panayotou *et al* 1997). On the supply side, environment-related technological change is driven by abatement costs and the ability of innovating firms to benefit from environmental damage mitigation (which in turn depends on the regulatory regime) and to appropriate the benefits from innovation with wider applications (which in turn depends on the intellectual property right regime). According to Johnstone (1997), in addition to these factors the level of industrial research and development is likely to be an important factor in the supply of

environment-relevant technological innovations. Indeed, Nentjes and Wiersma (1987) found that the most active industries in environment related R&D were the chemicals, petroleum and machinery and vehicles. Finally, environmental policy plays a key role in both the technological innovation. Clarity, predictability and stability of environmental policy are critical for the necessary investments to take place. Equally important is the flexibility of the policy instruments to allow firms to seek the least-cost methods of compliance, to take advantage of costs differentials in pollution abatement and to benefit from continuous innovation. In this regard, market-based instruments such as pollution taxes and tradable permits have significant advantage over command and control regulations. The case has also been made for a mixed system of pollution taxes to internalize the negative environmental externality of pollution *and* technologica innovation subsidies to encourage the positive technological innovation externality (Johnstone 1997).

Regulatory effects

The regulatory effects of trade liberalization on the environment arise from (a) improved environmental policies, standards and enforcement in response to economic growth from enhanced trade; (b) environmental measures included in trade agreements; and (c) relaxation of existing environmental policies due to specific trade pressures or restrictions on environmental policies by trade agreements. With regard to the first effect above, World Bank research based on data from 145 countries has found a positive association between economic growth and environmental regulation and security of property rights. With regard to the second effect, NAFTA demonstrates how trade liberalization can serve as a catalyst for improvements in both the level and the enforcement of environmental regulations. Trade agreements in general may promote harmonization of environmental standards and influence policies towards environmental subsidies and environment-related fiscal and trade measures. While the multilateral trading system encourages the use of international standards, and allows for higher levels of environmental protection, there is a widespread fear that trade liberalization and the resulting strife for competitiveness would "drag down" environmental standards in a race towards the bottom. There is no evidence that this has happened thus far.

Environment and Trade

Do environmental regulations act as barriers to trade? Do multilateral trade rules permit restrictions of trade for environmental purposes? Globalization in general and trade liberalization in particular has accorded previously purely domestic policies international importance. Included among such policies are competition policy, intellectual property rights and environmental policy. Furthermore, the reduction of tariff barriers has heightened the relative importance of non-tariff barriers as potential constraints on trade. At the same time, protectionist forces having lost the use of tariff barriers are inclined to focus their attention on non-tariff barriers. Environmental concerns, because of their emotive nature are a prime candidate. This in turn has raised concerns that some environmental measures might be disguised protectionism? Sorting out legitimate environmental policy from disguised protectionism is not easy. For example, some environmental regulations such a tax on imported large cars or a subsidy for pollution abatement afford protection to domestic producers and reduce imports. Multilateral trade rules make a fundamental distinction between (a) products standards and (b) process and production methods (PPM's). The two are treated very differently: national requirements on product standards and product-related PPM's are allowed, on non-product related PPM's they are not. We examine these in turn.

Product Standards

Multilateral trade rules permit national requirements for products to meet certain environmental, safety, and health standards provided that they are transparent and nondiscriminatory between domestic and foreign sources. Taxes and charges for environmental or other resources are permitted to be imposed on important products and to except exports as an application of the principle of national sovereignty. Border adjustments are permitted: the consumption of a product that can cause environmental damage may be taxed provided that the tax is applied in a transparent and non-discriminatory manner. Packaging and recycling requirements are more controversial as they are part of a domestic-focused waste reduction policy that can impose higher costs on importers; as such it is acting as a non-trade barrier to trade. The trade effects of this policy can be mitigated by giving advanced notice to allow foreign suppliers to adjust.

Given their direct impacts on trade, product standards are prime candidates for harmonization. Two agreements of the WTP system, the Agreement on Technical Barriers to Trade and the Agreement on Application of Sanitary and Phytosanitary Measure encourage harmonization of product standards and where possible, adherence to international standards.

Process and Production Methods

How natural resources are extracted or products are produced can have significant environmental impacts which countries attempt to control through harvesting restrictions, emission controls and specified production techniques. Extending such production-methods- 2 Based on Adams (1997). based standards (or taxes and charges) to imported products raise trade issues and conflict with the principle of national sovereignty: one country attempts to enforce a particular production method (that does not affect the final product) on another country. If the method of production affects the characteristic of the imported product, border tax adjustments are allowed under WTO rules, i.e. product-related PPM's are treated in the same way as product standards. Charges or standards on non-product related PPM's (i.e. on production methods that do not affect the product characteristics) violate the principle that "like products" must be accorded "like treatment," and are prohibited by WTO rules. Border tax adjustments or countervailing duties for non-product related PPM's are not allowed, i.e. the prices of imported products cannot be adjusted for the extra cost incurred by the domestic industry operating under such requirements.

Thus, differences in domestic environmental policies are seen as part of the many variations that constitute a country's comparative advantage and do not justify compensating levies or export rebates to offset price differences. Where trans-boundary and global environmental issues are concerned harmonization of non-product PPM requirements may be necessary, at least on a consensual basis, as in the context of regional or multilateral agreement. An interesting issue currently under consideration is the potential for using border tax adjustments in combination with domestic process taxes to reduce greenhouse gases (Adams 1997). In conclusion, unlike "product standards," "methods standards" are not candidates for harmonization; it would be both more difficult to do so and less beneficial. While some convergence is to be expected over time, production methods and solutions to local environmental problems are best tailored to local conditions. Yet the globalization of environmental concerns such as tropical deforestation and biodiversity loss pits the emerging product life-cycle perspective whereby consumers want to know the overall environmental characteristics of the products they buy against conventional notions of national sovereignty and of products as their physical characteristics (Adams 1997).

Does Environmental Policy Influence the Pattern of Trade?

Since differences in environmental policies and standards and their enforcement is translated into production cost differences, it is a legitimate concern that such differences may alter the pattern of trade. There is substantial evidence, however, that differences in environmental standards and environmental control costs have had very limited effect on trade patterns. The main reason is that environmental control costs are a very small fraction of production costs. Any comparative advantage created by lax environmental standards is overwhelmed by other sources of comparative advantage such as differences in resource endowments, technologies, human and physical capital, infrastructure and the macroeconomic policy environment. For example, Walter (1973) found that environmental control costs (ECC) amounted, on average, to 1.75% of the total value of US exports and 1.52% of US imports. Robison (1988) estimates the average EEC as a share of total exports as 0.37% in 1973 and 0.72% in 1982 and finds that a doubling in EEC sots has negligible impacts on output and trade; the trade balance is reduced by only 0.67%. Low (1992) has found that the traditionally lenient environmental standards in Mexico did not result in specialization in dirty industries. Grossman and Krueger (1993) found that pollution abatement costs in the US have not affected US imports from Mexico. If this is the case with Mexico and the US, which shares a long common border, have a large volume of trade, and have substantially different environmental standards, it is unlikely that environmental regulations have a significant impact on net exports in other cases either.

Another test of the relationship between environmental regulations and competitiveness is whether an increasing share of trade in pollution-intensive products comes from developing countries, which on the whole have more relaxed environmental laws (or more lax enforcement). While the share in world trade of pollution-intensive products from North America fell from 21 to 14 percent and that of Southeast Asia rose from 3 to 8 percent during 1965-1988 (Low and Yeats 1992), these trends are more indicative of increased demand for pollution-intensive products in newly industrializing countries than any shift of pollution-intensive production to developing countries.

Capital Flows, Foreign Investment and Environment

Capital flows in general, and direct foreign investment in particular, are major channels through which globalization impacts the environment. Foreign investment is a major vehicle of economic integration, technology diffusion and trade expansion. Globally, capital flows are larger than trade flows. Nearly 20 billion US dollars a day or 7 billion dollars a year cross national borders. Private capital flows to developing countries in 1996 were six times the official development assistance (ODA), accounting for 86 percent of the total capital flows to these countries (World Bank 1997). Unlike ODA, which has been steadily falling, private capital flows have been rising steadily right up to the recent financial crisis. Private capital flows are driven by the opportunity to earn a commercial return. These opportunities have increased considerably in the past decade as an increasing number of countries assume a greater market orientation and began to privatize state enterprises and to welcome foreign investment. However, private capital flows, being motivated by market opportunities rather than capital needs or developing priorities, tend to be concentrated in a dozen or so emerging economies and to avoid poor countries with high risk and undeveloped institutions and poor infrastructure. Moreover, private capital flows are not usually guided by sustainability considerations and are indeed very volatile and sensitive to changing market conditions. Furthermore, there is little information available about their environmental and social impacts. Of the nearly 280 billion US dollars of private capital flows to developing countries, 45 percent were accounted by foreign direct investment, 33 percent by debt finance and 19 percent by portfolio equity investments. Foreign direct investment (FDI) goes mostly into manufacturing plants, mining development, power stations, telecommunications, port development, airport and road construction, water supply, and sanitation, all of which have environmental and natural resource use implications. As such, FDI has the most direct and pronounced links to and effects on the environment and sustainable development. It is also a primary vehicle of technology transfer. Portfolio equity investments have only indirect links to the environment through their effect on the value of companies that they are directed to. If they build up the value of companies with high environmental performance, they have positive impacts; if instead, they put pressure for short-term profitability, they create disincentive for environmental performance. Debt financing or commercial lending to private companies gives the lender a stake in the borrower's financial performance, which may be affected by environmental risks. This is not usually the case with investors in government bonds since the governments' solvency is usually unrelated to its environmental performance (Gentry et al 1996). Private capital flows are highly concentrated. Developing countries received only about a quarter of global FDI and portfolio flows, and within the developing world, twelve countries in Asia, Latin America and Eastern Europe received 80 percent of the total flows to developing countries; sub-Saharan Africa, arguably the region with the greatest need for capital infusion, received only 2 percent of these flows. At the other extreme, China receives more than half of all FDI that goes to Asia and a third of the global capital flows to developing countries. What does the rapid growth of private flows mean for sustainable development? First, private capital flows are not a substitute for ODA, since poor countries that need them most attract the least. Moreover, private investment is not automatically channeled to sustainable development activities. To the contrary, the social and environmental areas traditionally have been among the activities least attracted to foreign investors, partly because of government regulations that limited foreign (and even domestic) private sector involvement. Moreover, without enforcement of environmental regulations and freedom to charge user fees or raise tariffs to cover costs (including an acceptable reform to capital), these sectors are not attractive to private capital. However, during the past five to seven years, a number of positive changes, such as deregulation, privatization, and financial innovation have increased the availability and attractiveness of these sectors to both domestic and foreign private capital. The development of innovative financing strategies such as build-own-transfer (BOT), build-own-operate (BOO), and build-own-lease (BOL), etc. have made it possible for the private sector to enter into infrastructure development, while the increased use of competitive bidding, coupled with environmental performance bonds or bank guarantees has improved the efficiency and environmental performance of FDI and hence its contributions to sustainable development. The past five years have witnessed a strong trend toward privatization of state-owned enterprises and public utilities, concessions to private developers of infrastructure inducing power generation, transportation, water supply and sanitation, and waste treatment, among others. The privatization of electric utilities in Argentina and concessions to private developers for public transport and waste management in Thailand and for water and sanitation in the Philippines are cases in point. Indeed, there is a clear trend in the 1990s of FDI shifting from resource extractive industries to environmental services that are generally more environmentally benign. The net effect of FDI and portfolio investment on the environment and sustainable development is difficult to determine in the absence of data and quantitative models. On the one hand, FDI provides risk capital that contributes to economic growth, employment and poverty alleviation; it also creates positive externalities in terms of increased competition, improved management skills, and access to greener markets and cleaner technologies. On the other hand, fears have been expressed that foreign direct investment gravitates toward countries with lower environmental standards or lax enforcement ("pollution haven" hypothesis).

Alternatively, capital mobility results in lower environmental standards as governments compete with each other to attract scarce investment by lowering environmental standards below efficient levels ("race to the bottom" hypothesis). On theoretical grounds, Bhagwati and Srinivasan (1997) argued that capital mobility does not lead to a "race for the bottom" if the economy is competitive and distortion free and there are no constraints on the use of tax instruments. Capital mobility does not enter a government's benefit-cost analysis calculus in choosing environmental standards if the first-best instrument of a tax or user fee is available and can be set equal to the cost that a firm's operations impose on the country. This cost includes the cost of providing public goods and services to the firm as well as the use of the environment for waste disposal (environmental cost). Weaker environmental standards may attract additional (foreign) investment but this will neither benefit nor harm the country since firms subject to an optimal (Pigovian) tax fully and efficiently compensate the country for any environmental cost associated with their investment (Bhagwati and Srinivasan, 1997). But of course, economies are neither fully competitive nor undistorted. The authors show that even monopoly power in capital and product markets does not destroy this benchmark efficiency; as long as the government can use tax instruments to exploit its market power, it is free to set its environmental policy efficiently. It is only when governments fail to tax capital efficiently that environmental policy becomes distorted; if governments overtax capital they may have an incentive to lower environmental standards to attract capital. Is there evidence that lax environmental standards actually attract more foreign investment? Repeated tests of the "pollution haven" hypothesis failed to find evidence of a systematic tendency of manufacturing plants to be located in countries with lax environmental standards. In choosing how much to invest and where, firms take into account many factors in addition to environmental regulations, such as size of the local market, the quality of the labor force, the available infrastructure, ability to repatriate profits, political stability, and the risk of expropriation. In this context, evidence indicates that the stringency or laxity of environmental regulations is insignificant as a determinant of location decisions. Indeed,

Wheeler and Mody (1992) found that multinational firms base their investment decisions primarily on labor costs and market access, while corporate tax rates and, by extension, environmental control costs play little or no role. In a World Economic Forum survey in 1997, 3,000 business executives from 53 countries were asked to rank environmental regulations and 26 non-environmental factors, ranging from government tax and investment policies to the quality of the workforce and infrastructure as to their role in their investment location decisions. The stringency of environmental regulations ranked 22nd.Data slows the importance attached to environmental regulations compared to 11 of the non-environmental factions. (A complete list of factors affecting industrial locations is given blow:

Industrial Location Factors Market-related factors Production-and-cost-related factors "Soft" location factors

- Proximity to market
- Preservation and/or expansion of market share
- Import restrictions and other trade barriers
- Developing of new market
- Avoiding foreign exchange risk
- Securing stable supply of raw materials and natural resources
- Social security contributions
- Skills of foreign labor force
- Business-related infrastructure
- Corporate taxes
- Energy costs
- Transport costs
- State Aids
- Obtaining technological knowhow
- Environmental stringency
- Political stability
- General social conditions
- Unionization
- Risk of strikes
- Public acceptance of new technologies
- Quality of living conditions

- Environmental quality
- Infrastructure for leisure activities

(Source: Springer, 1997.)

To the contrary, there is a growing evidence that foreign-owned firms or joint ventures tend to be cleaner than local firms (in general and state owned enterprises in particular) for at least five reasons: (a) the usually higher environmental standards of the developed countries are embedded in the technology of the overseas subsidiary (it is too costly to design different production processes for each location and regulatory regime); (b) they export to environmentally sensitive markets; (c) a degree of control is exercised by parent firms that do not want their image to be tarnished by environmentally irresponsible overseas operations; (d) in case of environmental accidents, they may still be subject to liability claims; and (e) pollution intensive industries happened to be among the least footloose industries. Furthermore, foreign investors exhibit a strong preference for a stable and predictable policy environment, which requires clear, transparent and consistently enforced environmental regulations approaching international standards. Having invested in the cleaner technology of the advanced countries, multinational firms have an incentive to lobby for higher environmental standards to raise the costs of their domestic rivals. Thus the cleaner technology of the multinational firms constitutes another argument for the liberalization of capital controls and encouragement of capital flow. Despite the likely positive influence of FDI on a country's environmental policy, the environmental performance of FDI cannot be taken for granted; it should be continuously monitored, as should that of domestic firms. FDI that is made in the absence of effective environmental policy, like any other type of investment, can result in environmental degradation, especially if the FDI flows are so large as to overwhelm the regulatory capacity of usually weak environmental authorities. are "most likely" to add to pollution and resource use even as they increase employment (and hence curtail resource encroachment) and reduce pollution arising from transboundary transport.

In conclusion, the overall net effects of a foreign direct investment on the environment and sustainability of host countries could be positive or negative. On the one hand, FDI generates employment, growth and wealth that makes larger investments in environmental protection possible, and it may even reduce pollution per unit of output through cleaner technology. On the other hand, it leads to increased industrial production and hence increased aggregate pollution levels (scale effect) as well as increased consumption of pollution goods such as electricity, fossil fuels for automobiles, etc. Since developing countries need both more investment and more improvements of their environmental performance, it behooves them to design a clear, transparent, stable and consistently applied environmental regulatory system that can serve as an attraction for foreign investors who want to be able to predict their costs and returns and to be assured that these costs are stable and common to all competitors.

"Most Likely" impacts of Foreign Direct Investment on employment and environment in OECD (home) countries
FDI outlaws

- Plant closure/relocation Reduction in local output; increase in imports of final products; increase in cross-border transport.
- Export substitution Reduction or change in the composition of output for export;
- Re-imports Reduction in output; increase in imports of final products; increase in cross-border transport
- Complementary exports Increase in output of intermediate goods or capital goods; increase in cross-border transport.
- Increased competitiveness Increase/no change in output; increase in cross border transport FDI inflows
- Mergers or acquisitions Shift in output; reduction in imports and cross-border transport

- Greenfield investment Increase in output; reductions in imports and cross-border transport
- Import substitution Increase in output; reductions in imports and cross-border transport
- Substitution of domestic production Shift in output
- Change in competitiveness Increase/no change in output for export; increase/no change in cross border transport

(Source: Springer, Rolf-Ulrich "Globalization, Employment and Environment" OECD Proceedings,
OECD Paris 1997).

In recognition of the growing importance of foreign direct investment, OECD has attempted to negotiate a multilateral agreement on investment (MAI) among its members and non-members willing and able to meet is obligations. (Argentina, Brazil, Chile, Hong Kong, and Slovak Republic joined the negotiations as observers.) MAI attempts to establish rules of investment and to create an inclusive investment climate, analogous to what has been negotiated and agreed upon for trade and services through GATT and GATS. The main objectives of a multilateral agreement on investment are to meet the foreign investors' need for (a) long-term stability of rules and procedures, (b) open markets and equal competitive opportunities with domestic investors, (c) protection of existing investments and (d) an international mechanism for settling disputes with national governments. OECD took the initiative of drafting MAI in recognition of (1) its major stake in investment rules, as it accounts for 85 percent of FDI outflows and 60 percent of inflows; (2) the common view of the benefits from free investment flows; and (3) its need for more comprehensive and effective rules. MAI was intended to include direct investments, portfolio investment, real estate investments and rights under contract. The main provisions of MAI were:.

- Non-discrimination: foreign investors must be treated no less favorably than domestic investors (National

Treatment) and all investors should be accorded the Most- Favored-Nation Treatment.

- Transparency of laws, regulations and procedures.
- Free transfer of funds to and from the host country
- Expropriation only for public purpose and with full compensation
- Dispute resolution through binding arbitration. General exceptions were allowed for national security, and integrity and stability of the financial system; temporary safeguards in response to balance of payments crisis; and country specific exceptions and regulations as negotiated among the parties. Exceptions for culture were also considered. With regard to the environment, MAI allowed freedom to governments to implement policies to protect the environment as long as these policies are not more stringent for foreign investors than for domestic ones, and MAI parties do not lower their environmental standards to attract foreign investment. The NAFTA provisions against environmental measures that constitute disguised restrictions on trade and investment were in effect expanded to include all OECD countries under MAI. MAI has been heavily criticized on a variety of fronts, from national sovereignty and cultural protection to public health and the environment. The environmental criticism included among others: (1) concerns that corporate challenges to environmental regulations will accelerate; (2) the intellectual property rights provisions giving patents full protection may conflict with provisions of the biodiversity convention; (3) while logging concessions are protected by MAI, acquiring land for preservation is not protected; and (4) governments are unduly constrained by provisions on rights from concessions, licenses, and permits in regulating corporations developing natural resources in their jurisdictions (Clarke 1998). At the end, MAI did not receive the necessary support from key parties to

come into effect. However, new efforts to negotiate a multinational agreement on investment are anticipated in coming years.

Globalization, Technology and Environment

Economic globalization affects both the nature and the rate of technological innovation and diffusion through a variety of channels: (a) more liberalized international trade, (b) more liberalized capital flows and a more favorable investment climate, (c) improved institutional and communication links, and (d) increased protection of intellectual property rights.

As we have already seen, 75 percent of international technology transfer arises from trade flows and 18 percent from investment flows (OECD 1995). Technology transfer arises from the trade of both goods and services including licensing of particular technologies through arms length transaction with foreign firms. Expanded trade also advances the rate of technological innovations by (a) enlarging the size of the market and generating economies of scale, (b) by realizing more monopoly profits from successful innovation and (c) by reducing dislocation of R&D efforts as protectionist barriers are removed. Capital flows, espsecially FDI, contribute to technological innovations and diffusion by (a) generating greater finance from capital exporting countries for financing investments in equipment, embodying more advanced technologies that are available in the host country, (b) by investing in R&D overseas, and (c) by generating technological spillover to national firms, through imitation, employment turnover, and by supplying multinationals demanding higher quality standards. For at least two reasons, the technology transfer by multinationals tends to be more advanced than what already exists in the host country: (a) 80 percent of FDI originates in countries that are primary sources of technological innovations such as the US, UK, Germany and Japan; (b) in order to overcome institutional, regulatory, cultural, and other hurdles in the host country, multinationals tend to apply advanced technology which, along with management, tend to be their most important competitive advantages (Grossman and Helpman 1995). It is estimated that 75 percent of industrial R&D is done by multinationals. Finally, the flow of technical expertise between countries encouraged by globalization results in international exchange of information which reduces the costs of developing new technologies. Archibugi and Michie (1995) report that 75 percent of patent applications in OECD countries come from outside OECD. However, again it is the middle-income and newly industrializing economies that have benefited most from the international flow of technology and knowledge. This creates a new source of inequality among developing countries as some converge technologically while others are left further behind. Having established the link between globalization and technological innovation and transfer, there remains to establish the link between technological change on the one hand and environmental quality and resource use on the other. What has been the environmental intensity of technological change? Evidences indicates that the material intensity of output in all regions of the world was reduced during the period 1970-1988. This includes most basic material inputs such as wood, metals, minerals, steel and raw agricultural materials: while world GDP during 1970-1991 increased by only 38 percent (Young and Sachs 1995) and CO2 dioxide emissions. This section draws heavily on Johnstone (1997). (WRI 1996) per unit of GDP also declined. This decline, or course, is only in part due to technological change; and in part to structural change. Furthermore, the aggregate resource use and pollution levels continue to rise as the scale effect of global output growth outweighs the structural and technological change effects. Is there a trend for technological innovations to be less environment-intensive or cleaner? Environmental intensity changes when there is a change in the product or the production process, when one input is substituted for another and when the technology is used more efficiently. There is no comprehensive analysis of recent technologies as to their environmental intensity.

In conclusion, globalization in principle could improve the environmental characteristics of technology through (a) increased exposure to foreign markets from where cleaner technologies and more effective pollution abatement equipment than those available at home can be imported; (b) increased access to export markets that may be more environmentally demanding than local markets; (c) foreign investment that brings with it the technologies and practices of the home country with more stringent environmental standards than the host country; (d) increased diffusion of the fast-growing export-oriented environmental goods and services industry. However, empirical evidence on the quantitative effect of globalization-driven technological innovation and diffusion, especially on developing countries, is extremely limited.

Intellectual Property Rights

One of the Uruguay Round results that liberalized trade and created the WTO was the Agreement on Trade-Related Aspects of Intellectual Property Rights, Including Trade in Counterfeit Goods, known as the TRIPS Agreement, which came into force with WTO on January 1, 1995. The TRIPS Agreement sets up the rules that WTO members must follow in establishing a system to protect intellectual property rights within their borders. Unlike other WTO rules that describe what countries may not do, TRIPS prescribes what countries must do. For example, it requires that any intellectual property rights granted to domestic innovators must also be granted to foreign innovators (*national treatment*) and no party should be favored over others (*non-discrimination*). Contravening the TRIPS Agreement may bring "cross-retaliation" through goods covered by other agreements. Developing country members and economies in transition have five years and less-developed countries ten years to set up the required laws and meet the standards set up in the TRIPS agreement. This is a challenge for countries that have no related legislation in place or have entire sectors developed based on imitations of innovations developed elsewhere (e.g. India's pharmaceutical industry). It is certain that complying with TRIPS will impose significant social and financial costs on countries through higher prices (due to payment of royalties and industry concentration). For example, small-scale seed and pharmaceutical companies in India and other developing countries are likely to go out of business and prices will rise beyond the reach of many poor people. TRIPS also is likely to have significant but not easily predictable effects on the environment. For example, concentration of the seed market in the hands of a few major producers who specialize in a few strains may result in loss of biodiversity and impoverishment of the genetic pool. The process of loss of thousands of land races that began with the Green Revolution would accelerate. A narrow genetic base and extensive monocultures will be more vulnerable to pests and blight epidemics. A related effect arises from the different treatment of formal and informal innovation. While varieties resulting from formal innovation resulting from scientific research by firms or individuals is protected under TRIPS, no protection is rendered to varieties produced informally by farmers by selecting the desired characteristics through traditional knowledge. This pits breeders' rights against farmers' rights and is criticized as unfair, especially since breeders and other formal innovators search for new crop traits and medicines by studying the products in use by traditional societies. As traditional medicines and land races developed over many generations do not fit the standard model of innovation, they are not protected by TRIPS, with the consequence that a steady flow of information from South to North worth billions goes uncompensated (Runnalls 1998).

Another concern relates not just to cultivated crops but to biodiversity in general. The release of new life forms, such as genetically modified plants, animals and microorganisms, protected by TRIPS, raises concerns relating to the ability of such "new life forms' to multiply mutate and migrate. Genetically modified organisms (GMO), once they have been released into the environment, may multiply and spread widely, affecting existing species. Even harmless GMOs without side effects may eventually mutate and assume unintended qualities or migrate to other organisms through pollination or sexual reproduction. Because of these concerns, the TRIPS Agreement allows for exceptions to patenting animals and plants, but the fact that countries can choose to patent life forms is considered contrary to the Precautionary Principle which is fundamental to sustainable development. These threats to biodiversity are expected to be addressed in the Biodiversity Protocol to the Convention on Biological Diversity now under negotiation.

Globalization and Environmental Policy and Performance

Economic globalization changes the "balance of power" between markets, national governments and international collective action. It enhances the influence of markets on economic, social, and environmental outcomes and reduces the degree of freedom and unilateral management capabilities of national governments, and it creates the necessity for states to cooperate both in the management of the global commons and the coordination of domestic policies (Zarsky 1997). Globalization creates market driven political pressures to gain or maintain competitiveness and this forces premature and not necessarily appropriate convergence of environmental policy. In the presence of diversity of environmental endowments, assimilative capacities and preferences efficient environmental management requires sensitivity to local ecological and social conditions. Diversity of conditions calls for a diversity of policies. Yet globalization leads to uniformity and inertia in environmental policy in the absence of collective action.

The main channel through which globalization influences environmental policy is through the cost of production. To the extent that environmental policy raises or is perceived to raise the cost of production, globalization-inspired concerns about gaining or maintaining competitiveness, mitigate against any change of policy, that might change the cost parameters unless competitors are subject to the same policy. This creates the inertia, pressures toward uniformity and a shift of power from national governments to market and global governance. Zarsky (1997) advanced the hypothesis that globalization creates forces that: (a) lead to domestic environmental "policy paralysis" and (b) puts the market in the driver's seat with regard to environmental policy and performance. On the one hand, diverse or weaker environmental policies raise concerns among competitors that the country is somehow trying to subsidize exports to attract foreign investors at their expense. On the other hand, any attempt to raise environmental standards raise concerns among domestic producers about higher costs of production and loss of competitiveness and hence loss of market share and foreign investment to competitors. Between the concerns of domestic producers and those of foreign competitors, environmental policy makers have a very narrow room to maneuver. This room has narrowed further as profit margins became smaller and smaller under the competitive pressures of globalization. Even if the increase in production costs is negligible and temporary, the fear or threat of being priced out of the market or lose a hard-won export market or foreign investment leads to "policy paralysis" and a strong bias towards the status quo. But the status quo does not favor the environment, since "relative market prices and patterns of competitive advantage usually grow out of an institutional context in which environment is left out of the equation. The pressures of globalization mean that improvements in environmental performance will be slow. Given the large new demands on global ecosystems posed by rapid economic growth in developing countries, slow progress—even if steady—points toward a pessimistic assessment of the prospects for global sustainability" (Zarsky 1997, p. 32) The pressures to maintain the status quo or make only small gradual changes in step with competitors is not a temporary phenomenon but one that gathers momentum over time: as the share of income denied from trade and foreign investment rises, the political pressures and lobbying not to disturb competitiveness intensify. This "Zarsky hypothesis" leads to a number of testable predictions. First globalization generated pressures to maintain competitiveness keep governments and enterprises from taking any initiatives to improve their environmental performance, if they entail significant costs on domestic producers. Second, developing country product standards will be slowly pulled up towards those of large markets and PPMs towards those of main competitors. Third, the benchmark-setting developed country standards will improve only slowly and gradually out of fear of loss of competitiveness to slowly converging developing countries. There has been no direct test of the Zarsky hypothesis and its predictions; Zarsky presents some indirect evidence that tends to support the hypothesis, at least in part:

- The proposed BTU tax in the US in 1993 was defeated on account of its perceived threat to US industry's international competitiveness despite the fact that (a) US energy prices are about one-half of those of the rest of OECD; (b) the estimated impact on even the energy intensive industries (aluminum, chemicals, fertilizers) was negligible (1-2 percent of the value of shipments); and (c) the economic and environmental benefits were assessed to be substantial in terms of deficit reduction, improved energy efficiency, decreased pollution and reduced dependence on foreign oil.
- The proposed EU-wide carbon/energy tax in the early 1990s was postponed indefinitely on the grounds that Japan, the US and other EU trading partners were not prepared to adopt similar measures. A similar greenhouse levy of on only $3 per ton of carbon was defeated in Australia in 1994 despite the exemption for transport fees and fossil fuel exports, and the estimated negligible impact on the other energy-intensive industries such as aluminum. The industry's contention that the perceived effects, however small, could drive investment away towards low-energy-cost countries carried the day.

- China, India, and many other developing and transitional economies which continue to subsidize fossil fuels and electricity to the order of 30-50 percent of the world prices are reluctant to remove these subsidies from fear of loss of competitiveness, despite the disappearance of the original rationale of these subsidies—the promotion of state-owned internal oriented industrial growth. The implication of the Zarsky hypothesis is that nation-states face a prisoner's dilemma with regard to environmental policy: pressures to compete for market and investments in a global economy compel them to pursue individual policies that result in lower pay-off than if they acted collectively. Cooperation and coordination of policy in internalizing environmental cost while recognizing the need for diversity would result in greater welfare for all countries. The absence of effective global governance or enforceable coordination condemns countries to a collectively suboptimal policy of premature and inefficient convergence to slowly improving environmental standards. Yet there are counter-threads that tend to improve environmental performance even as environmental policy is caught in classic prisoners dilemma. Growing public environmental awareness and rapidly spreading information about industry's environmental performance, both spearheaded by the information technology, give rise to a global environmental ethic. Under pressure from communities, customer, shareholders and employees, industry self-regulation is advancing ahead of formal regulations. Furthermore, the pressures of competition compel firms to intensify their search for more efficient, resource-saving, waste-reducing technologies. Moreover, the cross-border flows of capital, commodities, people and ideas promote technological and managerial change—resources are better allocated, cleaner and more efficient technologies are disseminated and the environmental standards of worst performers are gradually pulled up. These trends are fully consistent with the Zarsky hypothesis that globalization makes markets, the drivers of environmental performance, at the same time as it tends to "paralyze" official environmental policy.

Managing the Process of Globalization to Protect the Environment and Enhance Sustainability

Countries and people have the potential to drive significant benefits from the globalization process but there is still the problem of realizing this potential. Too much attention has been paid to the economic benefits of globalization and not enough to the social and environmental implications. As a result, the promise and potential of globalization as a force of sustainable human development may not be realized. Furthermore, at the same time that globalization improves the prospects for economic growth worldwide; it may reduce the economic prospects in individual countries, sectors and communities. A variety of factors contribute to wide disparities both within nations and between nations:

- Lack of access to more efficient technologies
- Lack of access to capital
- Inadequate flexibility to respond to changes in market demand
- Inability to manage structural change
- Weak institutions and absence of effective safety nets.

To the extent that globalization marginalizes economies, sectors, and people, it results in poverty-induced resource depletion and environmental degradation, which lead to further human deprivation, disparity and dispowerment. Globalization is likely to place significant stresses on the environment if perverse subsidies and other distortions are not removed and environmental costs fully internalized or if “social adjustment” policies are not in place to cushion economic dislocation and avert marginalization of the poor. Globalization, by driving a wedge between what is produced and what is consumed in any given locations alters the distribution of environmental impacts and the costs of avoiding them within the current generation and between the current and future generations. The environmental consequences of globalization differ from the economic effects both in time and space: (1) environmental impacts are more long-term, dynamic and cumulative and they are beset with uncertainty; we don't really know what the long-term damages are; and (2) environmental impacts involve both physical and non-physical spillovers that may or may not be transmitted through markets such as cross-border pollution, aesthetics, ethical or moral concerns of parties not involved in the transaction. Globalization generates international interest in what traditionally were considered purely domestic policies, since economic integration implies that trade and investment is now being affected by such policies. Globalization increasingly brings into conflict notions of national sovereignty over production processes with globally-oriented life-cycle perspectives, where consumers want to know the overall environmental impact of what they buy and consume.

In conclusion globalization brings with it potentially large benefits as well as risks. The challenge is to manage the process of globalization in such a way that it promotes environmental sustainability and equitable human development. The ability of nation-states to manage risks, inequalities and change is severely restricted by taxation constraints and the need to remain competitive. Hence, the traditional instruments of trade barriers and command and control regulations would not work because they would have unacceptably high costs in a globalized world and at the same time be less effective. To manage globalization in the interest of both people and the environment, it would be necessary to implement more efficient and innovative policies domestically and more effective global governance internationally.

National Policies

1. Accelerate democratization and institutional development to keep in pace with globalization
2. Increase accountability and transparency throughout the economy, and especially in the formulation and implementation of public policy
3. Channel more public investment to human capability formation
4. Preserve as much as possible of the autonomy of the state to exercise fiscal and monetary policies to achieve both macroeconomic stability and growth
5. Reform domestic policies that both distort trade and have negative environmental impacts (e.g. energy subsidies)
6. Correct existing market failures though efficient incentive systems (economic instruments) that internalize environmental costs, to avert their magnification by trade liberalization and economic integration.
7. Improve the effectiveness of environmental policy (benefit per dollar spent) through the involvement of businesses and local communities in monitoring and enforcement rather than relying on the state's limited budget and weak regulatory enforcement capacity. Instruments of empowerment include information disclosure in environmental performance of firms, and provision of training and other capacity building services to communities.
8. Institute social adjustment policies to cushion economic dislocation and avert the marginalization of the poor. It must be recognized, however, that the autonomy of the state to act deliberately to protect the environment or to cushion the impact on the poor of structural or other changes brought about by globalization is limited by the need to compete in the global economy for capital, jobs and markets, on the one hand, and by the interest that competitors and trade partners take on the country's domestic environmental and social policies, on the other. Countries facing financial crisis are further constrained by limitations imposed on their fiscal and monetary policy by creditors, the International Monetary Fund and the crisis itself.

International Policies

As we have seen, globalization constrains the state's unilateral management capacities and creates new imperatives for states to coordinate their domestic environmental policies as well as to cooperate in the management of the global commons. Without effective global governance (or effective multilateralism as Zarsky calls it) nation-states, subject to the pressures of globalization, drift towards a low-level environmental policy convergence that is insensitive to local ecological conditions and does not respect the diversity of preferences and priorities across and within nations. The challenge is to mobilize collective action among governments, firms and civil societies to overcome the gravity towards the sterile uniformity and inertia created by narrow competitiveness concerns and create a broader environmental policy framework, which will (a) recognize and allow for the diversity of environmental endowments and preferences; (b) raise the terms of environmental policy convergence; and (c) allow for continuous improvement in environmental performance. In such a framework policy coordination, harmonization and convergence would not be understood as homogenization or standardization of the objectives and instruments of environmental policy regardless of local circumstances, but a collective move towards sustainable development at different speeds depending on stage of development, environmental endowments, etc. Unfortunately, the one international "body" entrusted with the responsibility of building a bridge between environmental and trade policy, WTO's Committee on Trade and Environment (CTE), did not focus on finding "a synergy between environment and trade as two equal policy objectives. Rather they have explored how to fit environmental concerns within the framework of existing trade regimes" (Ewing and Taresofsky, 1996). CTE saw its role as one of limiting unilateral state actions in the name of environmental protection in order to protect the trading system rather than one of a paradigm shift from a negative to a positive trade-environment relationship and a "collective responsibility to promote sustainable trade, investment and growth (Zarsky 1991). Rather than focusing on how trade rules can promote sustainable development CTE focussed narrowly on (a) whether there should be a "safe harbor" within WTO for traderestricting measures included in multilateral environmental agreements (MEA); and (b) on whether eco-labelling schemes constitute non-tariff trade barriers. These issues are important as guidelines are urgently needed for both ecolabelling schemes and MEA negotiators but they cannot be resolved in isolation from other important issues in the interface of trade and environment and without an overarching framework of sustainable development in which both environment and trade are critically important and synergistic. As Zarsky (1997) put it, "first, the Organization [WTO] as a whole needs to affirm its commitment to a development agenda...Among other things, this would entail abandoning the idea that the primary goal of trade-environment diplomacy is to enhance the capacities of developed countries to restrict market access on environmental grounds (p. 41)."

Other unresolved issues besides MEA's and eco-labeling, central to the trade environment relationship are: (1) non-product-related process and production methods (PPMs) for which WTO rules have come increasingly in conflict with globally-oriented product life cycle perspectives; and (2) the gradual removal of domestic policies such as energy, chemical and water subsidies that both distort trade and damage the environment; and (3) internalization of environmental costs. The latter two issues, while domestic in nature and unilaterally beneficial are politically unpalatable because of concerns about loss of competitiveness, not unlike the concerns that limited unilateral trade liberalization and necessitated several rounds of trade negotiations and coordinated action, which culminated with the Uruguay Round. What is needed is a "Green Round" to coordinate joint action on the elimination of environmentally damaging subsidies and internationalization of environmental costs (with due recognition of diversity among countries). The question is whether WTO is up to the task of convening such a "Green Round" and coordinating the implementation of multilateral agreements on resource subsidies and internalization of environmental costs. WTO has thus far provided no evidence that is either prepared to view the trade-environment-relationship in a broader development context, or willing to address it in a more holistic manner.

A "Global Environment Organization" as called by Esty (1994) may be necessary to fill the gap which in its absence is now partially filled by regional groupings such as NAFTA, APEC, OECD and other, which attempt policy coordination among their members. That such regional initiatives are not a substitute for effective global governance and multilateralism can be seen from the now defunct efforts of OECD to negotiate a Multilateral Agreement on Investment (MAI) among is members. First, its main motivation was to promote foreign investor interests by reducing political risk and ensuring "national treatment" rather than to encourage investment for good environmental management and sustainable development. Second, it was met with suspicion by developing countries which viewed it as a run around WTO to conclude an agreement without their participation which, in letter, would bind only OECD members but in effect would apply to them as well. This gave rise to calls for exceptions to MAI provisions to protect the environment and ultimately for a much broader sustainable development investment agreement. Belated offers by OECD negotiators to include a "pollution haven" clause and to append environmental guidelines for multinationals did not constitute substitutes for effective policy coordination. Clearly, private capital flows into developing countries, especially emerging markets, will continue to grow rapidly into the foreseeable future. The challenge is to attract more foreign investment into the poorer countries and to direct it to sustainable development activities. In this regards, Official Development Assistance (ODA) has a critical role to play in leveraging private capital flows, both directly and through encouragement of better policies (including prudent macroeconomic policies and outward-oriented trade policies) in the recipient countries. Governments can ensure through regulations, incentives, and voluntary agreements that new investment is directed towards sustainable goals or, at a minimum, it does not jeopardize environmental, social and long-term development goals. At the multilateral level, there has been a clear trend since the early 1990s to take into account more consistently the environmental and social effects of projects. This is true of both the Multilateral Investment Guarantee Agency (MIGA) which guarantees funds to governments and the private sector to reduce risks, and the International Finance Corporation (IFC) that provides loans, equity and other financial instruments to private sector in development. In cooperation with national governments, international organizations should support the monitoring and the development of a database for tracking the environmental impacts of foreign capital flows on environmental quality and sustainability. With regard to technology, globalization can play a key role in generating and diffusing resource-saving and cleaner production technologies to developing countries but, for this to happen, several policy concerns must be resolved. First, the fact that developed countries dominate the generation of technological innovations, means that some of these technologies and their environmental features are ill-suited to the factor endowments, and economic and environmental circumstances of developing countries. Second, developing countries may lack the capacity to successfully absorb technological innovations, including those that aim to mitigate negative environmental impacts. It is, therefore, important that developing countries themselves develop their own institutional framework and capacity for adoption and adaptation of foreign technologies as well as for domestic generation of innovations (Johnstone 1997). Some domestic and foreign technological capacities tend to be complimentary than substitutable, domestic capacity should be coupled with removal of domestic barriers to diffusion of foreign technology, such as import tariffs on capital equipment, local content requirements, or foreign exchange restrictions. Lack of protection of intellectual property rights is another barrier to diffusion, since foreign firms may be concerned that transferring or licensing a technology may result in their losing their market advantage. Developing countries should undertake to increase their own capacity to assimilate transferred technology by fostering research and development, and improving their skills in negotiation and management with the aim to strengthen their intellectual property rights. International policies also have an important bearing on technology transfer. While MEAs such as the Montreal Protocol and the Basel Convention provide for transfer of best available, environmentally safe technologies to developing countries, care must be taken so that the transferred technology reflects the economic and environmental conditions of the recipient country rather than those of the donor (Johnstone 1997). For this to happen, it is necessary to develop cooperation between donors and recipient in R & D related to environmental technologies. Tropical environments and materials differ fundamentally from temperate ones in ways that affect the effectiveness and efficiency of environmental technologies designed for temperate environments.

Finally, there is scope for governments to ease the terms of access to some cleaner production technologies for developing countries as a form of development assistance. Technologies, such as newly developed vaccines or clean coal technologies which benefit diversity, the environment and human health, could be made freely available to developing countries. Developed countries can soften the impacts of TRIPs on developing countries by specifying very liberal terms of protection for environmental and clean production innovations involving public financing. There is a need for an Amendment or Understanding among WTO members that the rights of informal innovators are also protected and for a broader interpretation of TRIPs to include patents for land races and other products of traditional knowledge in exchange for a commitment by the developing countries to preserve these varieties. There are many innovative ideas including granting of special status, such as free or concessional access or royalty sharing, to source communities for commercial products "derived" from traditional knowledge or products in traditional use. The Convention on Biological Diversity already provides that the benefits from commercial use of genetic resources should be shared with the country of origin in a "fair and equitable way."

Finally, with regard to the risks posed to the biodiversity of flora and fauna, any patent protection afforded to the genetically modified organisms under TRIPs must incorporate the highest standards of protection according to the "precautionary principle," which is fundamental to sustainable development.

In conclusion, the more integrated environmental and trade policies are, the more sustainable economic growth will be and the more globalization can be harnessed for the benefit of the environment. At a rather modest level, this integration may take the form of institutionalization of environmental issues in future bilateral, multilateral and regional trade agreements. At a more ambitious level, new institutions of more effective and equitable global governance can be created to bring together governments, the private sector and civil society in a dialogue to achieve consensus for action in dealing with globalization-induced volatility, inequality and threats to environmental sustainability.

References

1. Adams, J. (1997). "Globalisation, trade, and environment." *Globalization and Environment,* OECD Proceedings, OECD: Paris.
2. Alexander Grant and Company. Various years. *Annual Study of General Manufacturing Climates of the Forty-Eight Contiguous States of America.* Alexander Grant and Company: Chicago.

3. Anderson, K. (1992). “Agricultural trade liberalization and the environment: A global perspective,” *The World Economy* 15(1): 153-71, January.
4. Anderson, K. and A. Strutt (1994). “On measuring the environmental impacts of agricultural trade liberalization,” Center for International Economic Studies, Seminar paper 94-06, University of Adelaide: Adelaide.
5. Archibugi, D. and J. Michie (1995). "The globalisation of technology: A new taxonomy," *Cambridge Journal of Economics* 19:121-140.
6. Bhagwati, J. and T.N. Srinivasan (1997). "Trade and the environment: Does environmental diversity detract from the case for free trade?" in Bhagwati, J. and Hudec, R., (eds), *Fair Trade and Harmonization: Prerequisites for Free Trade? Vol. 1: Economic Analysis* MIT Press: Cambridge, MA.
7. Clarke, T. (1998). “MAI-Day! The Corporate Rule Treaty: The Multilateral Agreement on Investments (MAI) seeks to consolidate global corporate rule,” http://www.nassist.com/mai/mai(2)x.html.
8. Epping, M. (1986). "Tradition in transition: The emergence of new categories in plant location," *Arkansas Business and Economic Review,* 19(3):16-
9. Esty, D.C. (1994). *Greening the GATT, Trade, Environment, and the Future,* Institute for International Economics: Washington, DC.
10. Ewing, K.P. and R.G. Taresofsky, (1996). *The "Trade and Environment" Agenda: Survey of Major Issues and Proposals form Marakesh to Singapore.* IUCN Environmental Law Centre, Bonn, December.
11. Gentry, B.S. *et al* (1996). *Private Capital Flows and the Environment: Lessons from Latin America.* Yale Center for Environmental Law and Policy (draft report).
12. Grossman, G.M. and E. Helpman (1995). "Technology and trade." *CEPR Discussion Paper* 1134: London.
13. Grossman, G.M. and A.B. Krueger (1993). "Environmental impacts of a North American Free

Trade Agreement." In P. Garber (ed.) *The US-Mexico Free Trade Agreement.* MIT Press: Cambridge, MA, 13-56.

14. Grossman, G.M. and A. Krueger (1995). "Economic growth and the environment," *Quarterly Journal of Economics* 110(2): 353-77, May.
15. Henriques, I. and P. Sadorsky (1996). "The determinants of an environmentally responsive firm:
16. An empirical approach," *Journal of Environmental Economics and Management,* 30: 381-95.
17. Hoffman, U. and D. Zivkovic (1992). "Demand growth for industrial raw materials and its determinants: An analysis for the period 1965-1988." *UNCTAD Discussion Paper No. 5*: Geneva.
18. Johnstone, N. (1997) "Globalization, technology, and environment." *Globalization and Environment,* OECD Proceedings, OECD: Paris.
19. Levinson, A. (1997). "Environmental regulations and industry location: International and domestic evidence," in in Bhagwati, J. and Hudec, R., (eds), *Fair Trade and Harmonization: Prerequisites for Free Trade? Vol. 1: Economic Analysis* MIT Press: Cambridge, MA.
20. Low, P. (ed.) (1992). "Trade and the environment: A survey of the literature,", in Low, P. (ed.) *International Trade and the Environment.* World Bank Discussion paper 159, The World Bank: Washington DC.
21. Low, P. and A. Yeats (1992)., "Do 'dirty' industries migrate?" in Low, P. (ed.) *International Trade and the Environment.* World Bank Discussion paper 159, The World Bank: Washington DC.
22. Lucas, R., P. Wheeler and H. Hettige (1992). "Economic development, environmental regulation
23. and international migration of toxic pollution 1960-1988,: in Low, P. (ed.) *International Trade and the Environment.* World Bank Discussion paper 159, The World Bank: Washington DC.
24. Lyne, J. (1990). "Service taxes, international site selection and the 'green' movement dominate executives' political focus." *Site Selection,* October.

25. Nentjes, A. and D. Wiersma (1987). "Innovation and pollution control," *International Journal of Social Economics,* 17(4): 247-65. OECD (1995). *Foreign direct Investment, Trade and Employment.* OECD: Paris. OECD (1996). *Globalizaiton of Industry: Overview and Sector Reports.* OECD: Paris. OECD (1994a). *The Environmental Effects of Trade,* OECD: Paris. OECD (1997). *Globalization and Environment,* OECD Proceedings, OECD: Paris.

26. Panayotou, T. (1997). "Demystifying the Environmental Kuznets Curve: Turning a Black Box

27. into a Policy Tool." *Environmental and Development Economics,* 2(4): 465-484.

28. Panayotou, T. (1997). "Taking stock of trends in sustainable development since Rio." In *Finance for Sustainable* Development*: The Road Ahead:* Proceedings of the Fourth Group Meeting on Financial Issues of Agenda 21, pp. 35-72, Santiago, Chile. United Nations, New York.

29. Panayotou, T. and J.R. Vincent. (1997). "Environmental regulation and competitiveness." *Global Competitiveness Report,* World Economic Forum: Geneva.

30. Panayotou, T., T. Schatzki and Q. Limvorapitak. (1997). "Differential Industry Response to Formal and Informal Environmental Regulations in Newly Industrializing Economies: The Case of Thailand." A Case Study for the HIID Asia Environmental Economics Policy Seminar.

31. Pargal, S. and D. Wheeler (1995). "Informal regulation of industrial pollution in developing countries." *World Bank Policy Research Working Paper* 1416. World Bank: Washington, DC.

32. Repetto, R. (1993). *Trade and Environment Policies: Achieving Complemntarities and Avoiding*

33. *Conflicts,* World Resources Institute: Washington, DC.

34. Repetto, R. (1995). *Jobs, Competitiveness, and Environmental Regulation: What are the Real Issues?* World Research Institute: Washington, DC, March.

35. Robison, H.D. (1988). "Industrial pollution abatement: The impact on the balance of trade." *Canadian Journal of Economics* 21(1).
36. Runnalls, (1998). "Shall we dance?" International Institute for Sustainable Development (IISD), Trade and Sustainable Development Research Guide, http://iisd1.iisd.ca/trade/dance.htm
37. Schmenner, R. (1982). *Making Business Location Decisions.* Prentice-Hall: Englewood Cliffs, NJ.
38. Smith, K. and J.A. Espinosa (1996). "Environmental and trade policies: Some methodological lessons" *Environment and Development Economics*: 19-40.
39. Sprenger, R.U. (1992). *Umweltschutz als Standortfaktor.* Friedrich Erbert Stiftung: Bonn.
40. Sprenger, R.U. (1997). "Globalization, employment and environment" *Globalization and Environment,* OECD Proceedings, OECD: Paris.
41. Stafford, H.A. (1985). "Environmental protection and industrial location," *Annals of the Association of American Geographers,* 75(2):227-240.
42. Strutt, A. and K. Anderson, (1998). "Will trade liberalization harm the environment? The case of Indonesia to 2020." Seminar Paper 98-04 Center for International Economic Studies, University of Adelaide, May.
43. Subramanian, A. (1992). "Trade measures for environment: A nearly empty box?" *The World Economy,* January, 15(1). United Nations (1996). *World Economic and Social Survey,* UN: New York.
44. von Moltke, K. (1996). "International environmental management, trade regimes and sustainability." Paper prepared for the International Institute for Sustainable Development Winnipeg, Manitoba, Canada, January.
45. Walter, I. (1973). "The pollution content of American trade," *Western Economic Journal,* 11:61-70.
46. Wheeler, D. and A. Mody (1992). "International investment location decisions: The case of US firms," *Journal of International Economics,* 33: 57-76.

47. Wintner L. (1982). *Urban Plant Siting*, Conference Board: New York.
48. World Bank (1997). *Can the environment wait? Priorities for East Asia.*
49. World Resources Institute (1990). *World Resources 1990-91*, Oxford University Press: New York.
50. World Resources Institute (1996). *World Resources: A Guide to the Global Environment.* WRI: Washington, DC.
51. World Trade Organization (1995). *International Trade Trends and Statistics*, WTO: Geneva.
52. World Trade Organization (1996). *Trade and Foreign Direct Investment.* WTO: Geneva.
53. Young, J.E. and A. Sachs (1995). "Creating a sustainable materials economy," in L. Brown *et al*, (eds.) *State of the World 1995*. Earthscan: London.
54. Zarsky, L. (1991). *Trade-Environment Linkages and Ecologically Sustainable Development*, Report to Department of Arts, Sports, Environment, Tourism and Territories, Environmental Strategy Branch, Australia, October.
55. Zarsky, L. (1997). "Stuck in the mud? Nation-states, globalization, and environment." *Globalization and Environment*, OECD Proceedings, OECD: Paris.

About the author

Mr. Shabeer Ahmad Bhat was born on 11 April 1988 in a village namely Okey which is four kms away from the main district Kulgam of South Kashmir. He received his primary, secondry education from a government school and completed his graduation in 2008 from Govt. Degree College Kulgam. By then he got admission in the University of Kashmir and pursued his M.A. in Sociology from the department of Sociology university of Kashmir. He has qualified UGC NET, SET, as well. He is pursuing his research in the department of Sociology under the supervision of Dr. Pirzada Mohammad Amin who is also the head of the department of social work. Shabeer Ahmad is working on the specialized area of Sociology of Religion with specific reference to Hindu pilgrimage tourism in Relation to mother Goddesses of Shri Mata Vaishno Devi shrine. Shabeer Ahmad has more than ten publications of national and international repute as well. Besides he has attended many national and international conferences in many parts of the Indian sub continent.

www.ingramcontent.com/pod-product-compliance
Lightning Source LLC
Chambersburg PA
CBHW060254290526
45789CB00001B/331
9781499643695